Say Hello to Heaven

Developing Your Psychic
and Mediumship Abilities

Sarah Janik
*Bridging the Physical
and Non-Physical Worlds*

Editing by Leya Booth
Interior Layout by Steven W. Booth, Genius Book Services

ISBN: 979-8-218-43894-4

240627

Contents

INTRODUCTION

"The greatest discovery in life is self-discovery. Until you find yourself you will always be someone else. Become yourself."
~ Myles Munroe

My first encounters with spirit began as a young girl. Waking up at night, I felt spirits around me. Often, I would see them. I could distinguish men from women, children from adults, but as a child, I lacked the curiosity to discern whether the presence was someone I knew who was connected to me, or if they were just connected to the house I lived in at the time. Physically, I felt the hair on my arms stand up, and this sensation frightened me. I wanted nothing more than for them to go away. I had no curiosity as to why they were visiting me.

As I grew up, an elderly man who I often felt and saw in several different houses paid me many visits. He knew I could sense him. By then, I'd had lots of experiences hearing, seeing, or feeling the presence of spirits around me, in every house, and always just shrugged it off. I began to believe that everyone had experiences with spirits like I did, and that everyone just chose not to talk about it because it was taboo. I thought everyone kept these experiences close to them for fear of judgment by others.

Because I was preoccupied with my friends and growing up during my teen years, I quite literally began pushing my abilities away, as I wanted nothing more than to fit in. The effect was that my experiences were much fewer during this period in life. Deep down though, I still knew that I was different and sensed things more than my friends did. I just wasn't ready to accept it.

But then I started to have *different* kinds of experiences. During that period of time in my life, I began feeling and picking up on the energy of those in the living. I would walk into a room, or be around groups of people, and genuinely feel and *know* what they were going through. Even the people that appeared to have it all together. I could feel the things they stuffed down and held back. I was like a giant receiver— feeling the thoughts and emotions of those I cared for or empathized with. I hated seeing kids being picked on. I had to say hi, smile or wave at them because it made my heart sink as I could feel just how they felt. I wanted to help. In large gatherings, I mistook what I would later understand to be my gifts as social anxiety, because I felt such overwhelming energy. I later realized that the energy I was feeling wasn't my own anxiety; rather, I was being overwhelmed by the combined energy of large groups of people, not knowing that I could control what I was experiencing. Sensing and feeling everyone's emotions and emotional baggage without a filter can be quite overwhelming, to say the least. If you are someone who also feels this way, know that you are not alone. Many sensitive people feel they may have anxiety in crowds when they are simply feeling the energy of the room. Later, I'll talk more about tips on how to deal with empathy overwhelm so that you, too, can filter out experiences you chose not to be a part of.

From a young age, I knew I wanted to help people, and so I began my career in healthcare in my late teens, eventually becoming a registered nurse. I believe our souls sign up for jobs here on Earth to accomplish certain tasks. Healing myself and then others is one of mine, but you don't have to be a healer to contribute to society. Remember that we need all kinds of people to work together as a whole to accomplish the bigger picture. I believe if you are reading this, you more than likely have some kind of soul journey involving healing to overcome some feat that we deal with as humans. Once you've healed any given situation that you've gone through in life, you then can help others through the same thing. It's not an obligatory thing, but more of a contribution to the whole. I know that my destiny is to help people, whether physically, mentally, or spiritually—the living, and those in spirit. In my twenties, I was able to turn my focus back to me—to having a family and raising my children and reconnecting with my life again, which opened new doors. I began to realize just how little others' perceptions of me really mattered. I hadn't yet mastered this but opening to it started to shift things in my life.

After I had my first son, I began to have more experiences with spirit once again. One night, I saw a man enter my room, slowly walk over to my son's crib, and look over the edge at my sleeping baby. The man was transparent, but a full body figure with slight detail was visible. The man was calm and protective in how he carried himself. I knew my son was safe because of how the man was watching over him. The man's presence and actions were a message to me in and of itself. However, even though he was benevolent, I was uncomfortable *seeing* him, and I started sleeping with the covers pulled up over my face to try and prevent myself from seeing more of these visits.

One night, while I was still a nursing student and home alone, busy with homework and taking care of my young children, I felt extremely overwhelmed by it all. Trying to keep up with nursing school, dinners, chores, and spending time with my children was a lot for a young mom, as my children's dad was away a lot with work. I was in bed, stressed about life, running though all of the to-do's, and for the first time, I *heard* spirit aloud. A man called out my name in a deep voice as if trying to get my attention. "Sarah!"

Without a doubt, there was no one home but me and my little ones. No one was awake but me, and there was certainly no man in the house. To hear the voice of someone you clearly know is not among the living is terrifying. Yet somehow, I had a deep sense of knowing that this was a spirit who obviously knew me and who I was. For one, he knew my name, and two, he was around me and during this stressful time trying to interrupt the obvious shenanigans running through my mind. Was he trying to help in some way? It worked. All the stress that seemed to be so overwhelming started to melt away. It took my attention off the things we so often preoccupy our mind with when we have nothing else going on. It brought me back to the present. It reminded me that we are not alone, and somehow, as scary as it was, I knew he was helping me refocus my attention and relax, just as a parent or someone would do to help ease any stressors for their child.

Ever since I was a young girl, I've had a strong knowing that spirit is real. It wasn't something anyone taught me; it was more of a knowing. We are souls, and there is an afterlife. In my twenties I began to see that these experiences I had in life were not something that happened to everyone. I understood that much by this point. But now I began to see that just maybe, I had a gift. I was much more in tune with the other side than the average person. Every house I ever lived in provided at least one experience, if not many. Hearing, seeing, feeling, and smelling spirit were all part of my existence, but hearing my name called out was new. I remember another time feeling my grandmother in spirit lay her hand on my left shoulder to comfort me during another stressful moment. I still remember that like it was yesterday. If you've had such encounters, you know it's not something you easily forget. I knew it was her the second I felt someone lay their hand on my shoulder. I smelled a smell that I can't even describe, but I know that if I smell it, it is no one other than my grandma. I also remember seeing her so clearly in my mind's eye. But I didn't think I could hear the voices of the deceased out loud. It had never dawned on me until this point. Thinking about all of my experiences was making me start to feel a way about my own abilities. Did I have a connection? Why had I had so many experiences? Did everyone else really experience this after having a loved one pass?

Several years into my nursing career, I started receiving visits from my departed patients. I began to notice that the visits I got were from those who had really left an impression on me, or whom I had a close connection to. They appeared to me as full-bodied apparitions, at home or when I was going about my business during the day, just prior to going to work my shift, only to discover that they had in fact passed away. I continued to get visits from patients who had passed away and would receive information about them that I hadn't known prior to their passing, until I would later look them up. Sometimes it was the date of passing, or the birth year, and sometimes it was a name that I couldn't remember in my waking life for the sake of me. Sometimes it was health-related information regarding an illness they may have dealt with at the time of their passing.

I began to have more detailed dream visits of those that had passed tragically and not gotten closure around their deaths. A young boy came to me telling me he was from Encinitas, Ca. He then showed me a massive and muddy landslide that caused huge chunks of rock to break off and roll down the hill into the valley. He told me his name. The next week, a young girl from the New England area came to me. She had long blonde hair and was outside riding her bike when she was kidnapped. I asked her name, and she replied with such clarity. I was shaken by these experiences when I was able to get online and google the exact names and locations, seeing that I was truly visited by these souls. Early on, when spirits started visiting me more frequently, I remember having a dream of being in the music room of my junior high school and hanging out with a classmate. We were talking about connecting to the souls of the departed. It took me several years to realize he was visiting me in that dream and that he too had passed away. A couple of years passed, and I started seeing this classmate in my mind's eye. It happened several days in a row, and I heard his first name aloud. I knew I was seeing him as I had seen other spirits. I had forgotten his last name but knew I needed it to be able to look him up and see if he had also passed. I remembered the dream of the girl and that she responded to me when I asked her name. I told him I needed his last name if he wanted to help me get confirmation of his visit. That afternoon, I sat down to watch television and saw a hand just above my TV writing out his last name on a chalk board. I looked him up. Unfortunately, he had passed away from cancer just a couple of months prior to my dream. It was then that I realized the dream I had of him was a visitation. We had speech class together in the music room I dreamed of him in.

Then came a time where I went through a bit of a spiritual awakening. Have you ever hit a wall in life and felt like nothing was working out, where things started to fall apart, and you were left wondering what the purpose of life is? Many people will go through this in life at different times (maybe a midlife crisis, or many empty nesters and retirees also go through this). *Who am I? What is my purpose? How have I been living out of alignment? Why have I been living so outside of my authenticity for the sake of others? Why do I feel the need to always show up for others first? What truly makes me happy? How can I live in more joy?* Some people put so much time into their job that it becomes who they are. They then retire or lose their job and feel completely lost, only to realize they don't know who they are outside of that identity. *Who am I without my job, or being a parent or a spouse?* I'm not saying don't put energy and time into these things. They are amazing and part of life's greatest joys. I'm saying don't forget about *you*. In the end, we get to revisit these questions during a life review, to see how well we were also able to honor and love ourselves, and to see how well we were able to do the same for others.

During this time, spirit revealed that it wasn't just okay to be experiencing these things, but that it was part of my soul's purpose. It was an inner knowing that continuing to live any other way would keep me stuck in a place I didn't want to be. Regardless of anyone's opinion of me, it was time to express this part of myself that I had worked so hard at hiding my entire life. It was one of the things I wanted more than anything, to be authentically myself, regardless of anyone else's perceptions. It was at that time that I began to experience nightly visits. I could feel myself surrounded by people's loved ones and my loved ones in spirit, and I received dream visits from practically everyone I had known who had passed away during my lifetime.

During this time of revelation, a childhood friend who had passed tragically in an accident visited me twice in one night. In my dream, we were hanging out in his living room, and he looked at me and asked me to tell him his birth date. He had a calendar and was flipping through it, and as I guessed the dates he asked of me, he turned the calendar around to show me that I was correct. Later on, I ended up looking into this to find out if the dates were correct, as I didn't remember in my waking life. They were.

He was trying to get me to say the things I was picking up on just like I had seen mediums do on television. Upon waking, with the limited illumination of the night, I was able to see him standing right next to my bed. He leaned over me to make sure that I saw him, and I knew at that moment he was delivering a huge message to me about connecting more deeply with my abilities. He had come to show me I could use my abilities to connect to spirits and help people connect to their loved ones to provide healing. Since then, I have experienced many visits from him, always right when I need a pick-me-up or a reminder to live a bit more fully, as that was who he was at his core. He was fun and spunky, and he reminded everyone around him that life was meant to be lived fully, in a way that many forget.

I no longer needed convincing. Having these experiences really began to intrigue me. It added to my desire to help bring healing to others and to show them that our souls live on after we leave the physical world. Passing away is only the change from physical to nonphysical, a time when our souls leave behind our physical bodies and the material world—a shedding or transformation, if you will. Energy can never truly die; science has proven this much.

Being a nurse has also introduced me to medical intuitive information that comes through in readings. My career in nursing and my abilities as a medium are linked and have aided in the assistance that I am able to offer to help people live fuller, healthier, happier, more joyous lives while they are on Earth.

Working in healthcare for twenty-plus years has shown me that spirit is here and waiting to greet us, even before we cross over. Numerous times, I've witnessed patients close to death who start seeing their mom, dad, and loved ones who have crossed over. Yes, pets also await us, as they very much have souls as well! This happened frequently while I was working at my first healthcare job in assisted living. Even though that was many years ago now, from time to time, I still have visits from some of those patients. The connections we make with people truly last a lifetime!

Many of those who have a near-death experience mention entering a completely different world and consciousness, experiencing tremendous feelings of love that we would struggle to understand here in the physical world. In the book *Dying to Be Me*, written by Anita Moorjani, she mentions leaving her body and floating above while being able to see herself in the hospital room, where the doctors were working on her physical body, and seeing and hearing the conversation the doctors were having about her down the hall in a different room. She was also able to see her brother on an airplane rushing to see her at the hospital. Moorjani and all the others say all it requires to travel from place to place is your own thoughts, and that you can be drawn in by people simply thinking of you. Spirit has confirmed this to me in readings as well. If you want your loved one to step in, simply send out a thought. They can hear you. This movement without a body is something we can only dream of on this physical plane. It's hard to comprehend when all you remember is being bound to your physical body and having to travel by plane, train, or automobile. This confirms that if our souls can be in more than one place at a time, they are also with more than one earthbound loved one at a time.

Once we cross over, our souls may help others here on Earth. What you do on the other side depends on what you do or have completed here. This is one reason readings should be limited to no more than every three to six months. Souls are not just waiting around for us to connect with them 24/7. They have roles to complete and need time to develop and grow on a soul level as well. I have found that many helper souls (guides and angels) are those who have lived many lifetimes and no longer choose to come back to Earth, as they have no more humanness to work on. Children and those who pass young are often helper souls as well. They often teach people how to open their hearts and experience joy in a way that other connections may not. You know what I mean if you've had or met a child, but felt they carried the knowledge of someone much older than you.

Aside from what souls undergo, people need time between readings to live, learn, heal, and experience life. After losing a loved one, it can be tempting to want to connect with them on a regular basis. However, it is important to have time to grieve and heal, and to learn how to reexperience all of the beautiful thing's life has yet to offer us in this world while we are still here.

Healing takes time. I have seen some amazing transformations take place in people from reading to reading, and I see how much connecting people to their loved ones helps them to be able to live a freer, more peaceful life. There have been times when I have seen such a weight lifted off someone's shoulders after a reading that would have taken years of counseling to achieve in comparison. In fact, I've been told that very thing by many people. The reassurance that their loved ones still exist, are by their side, and most definitely will be waiting for them can be enough to help shift their perspective, helping them understand that they are here for a reason, that it is okay to still live while experiencing grief.

With that being said, it's important to mention that many people will also need grief counseling. Spirit has even brought this up in readings to try to further help their loved ones heal. Mediumship is not a replacement for professional grief or mental health counseling, but it can be a great adjunct therapy that helps in the healing process. I have even had quite a few people referred to me by therapists, and I believe the combination of the two can be a great aid in the grieving process. Mental health is such an important part of our overall health and assists us in living life more fully. I always recommend following your heart and intuition. You know what healing modalities are best for you. Mediums are just one way to help bring light and healing to this world.[1]

If you are reading this, it's safe to assume that you are interested in learning more about the afterlife or tuning in to your own abilities. My goal is to help you understand that we all innately carry the ability to pick up on and tune in to the living and those on the other side. We are spirit. It is our God-given ability as soul bearers.

Using your abilities as an intuitive, psychic or medium is quite literally allowing your soul and energetic body to surface in your humanness. You

---

1 I may use the words *psychic* and *medium* interchangeably. While psychic abilities are tuning into the living, and mediumship abilities are tuning into spirit, they work similarly. You tune into and pick up the information needed to help in a reading, whether you choose to work on your psychic abilities, mediumship abilities, or both.

are so much more than a human body with a brain. You have the ability to connect to source, spirit and all of its wisdom.

Remember, just as with any skill, it takes time and continued focus to grow. No one starts out giving full-blown readings. But if you follow along and continually use the exercises and recommendations in this book, and make a commitment to stick to them, you will see that your abilities will grow.

Part One:
What's It All About?

CHAPTER ONE

Developing Your Psychic and Mediumship Abilities

"Life doesn't end with the body's death.
The soul continues its journey beyond this life."
~ Author Unknown

Mediumship is the communication between the physical world and the spirit world. Psychic work is connecting to the souls of living people, places, or events. I believe that anyone can be a medium or a psychic. We are human, but we are also spirit, so we all naturally have the ability to do this. Many mediums have had experiences with spirit since early in life; others have had their abilities open up later in life. But it can also be taught and learned. I have witnessed both ways firsthand.

Many people are drawn to mediumship or psychic development because they have a natural pull toward it and have had prior experiences before any growth of their abilities. Most people I have met who are having these experiences feel they have been led to it. Others have had a life-changing experience, such as trauma, loss, or a near death experience, which may have opened their connection with spirit.

Everyone's journey is different, and not everyone feels drawn to being a medium, just as not everyone feels called to be an NFL football player or a professional artist. If you feel drawn to the metaphysical world, and you're interested in mediumship or the paranormal, please trust that this interest is calling to you for a reason. Only you know your experiences, and you must determine what that reason looks like for you. That is the beauty of life: we get to decide what we want to create for ourselves. We are all much more connected to God, the Universe, or whatever creative force you believe in than most people think. Whether you choose to do this just for yourself, to help connect you to your own loved ones in spirit, or pursue it professionally, that is up to you. Nothing is outside of your ability.

The belief that you can't do something, or that only "special people" carry these abilities is what prevents you from accomplishing any role or job you want to achieve in life. I do believe people are usually led toward or have interest in different psychic modalities because of their intrinsic abilities. I have met many mediums over the last decade, and each one is different.

Many people choose to develop their intuition simply so that they can navigate their own lives with more ease. Once you begin trusting your intuition, decision-making becomes much easier. When you learn to trust yourself, you can separate intuition from fear and worry. If you have any self-doubt, let me tell you that I had a teacher, early on in my mediumship development, who had never had any prior experiences with spirit in her life before she started, but she went on to become an amazing medium and teacher of mediumship.

When developing your gifts, consistency is key. Committing to weekly practices, exercises, and readings works best. You will see over time how much you will grow, and you'll become much more confident in your abilities to connect to spirit or perform psychic readings, if that is what you choose. Many compare these gifts to muscle memory. Development takes time, and it doesn't happen overnight. Your abilities get stronger the more you use them, just like with any other skill in life. Likewise, if you don't commit and put in the work, then you probably won't see much growth in your abilities. As with any skill, you get out what you put in.

It is also important not to take yourself too seriously. Joy and fun should be incorporated into your development, as well as taking time for living your life here on Earth. Sometimes people believe that to be spiritual, you must stop doing certain things that make you human in order to properly connect to spirit. They believe you should eat only healthy foods, and you can't drink alcohol or swear. That just isn't the case. Spirit doesn't expect perfection because spirit isn't perfect. There is no such thing as perfection, and that is the beauty of existence.

As I mentioned before, spirit wants to help us connect so they too can help bring us peace, so we can live freer, more joyful lives. Living your life is important. Being you, whatever that may entail, is the most important thing you can do. So, have fun in your development!

It is generally said that we all have these abilities as young children, but as we grow up and go to school, we're taught what is "appropriate" and what is not. At this point, around grade school, we start to close off experiences that are labeled as "abnormal." Sometimes children are overwhelmed because they lack the ability to tune out what others routinely ignore, and they choose to close off rather than deal with this.

Similarly, people who experience loss, trauma, or a near-death experience may struggle to tune out spirit or psychic abilities because their nervous systems have been so overwhelmed that they are broken wide open. These events lead people to be hyper-aware in situations, almost as a self-protective mechanism. They need to feel okay or safe, so their nervous system literally learns to tune in even more. Think of it like your five senses on steroids: hearing, seeing, feeling, and picking up on things from those living and in spirit that others don't.

It is the same for people who have lost a person close to them. This may also be a time when they start to experience spirit more. Grief is a strong emotional experience. The loss of a loved one does the exact same thing to your nervous system. Trauma and loss may both lead to our senses being more tuned in than the average person's under typical conditions.

Many people also intentionally connect to their loved one in spirit because they are longing for reconnection. For example, someone who loses their spouse may notice after their loved one is gone that they start to sense the presence of their spouse at times. Many find they start receiving information without even trying, and they find themselves tuning into their abilities, not only for their own healing and connection, but to help others who have been through similar experiences.

Another common path to intuitive abilities is through a near-death experience. This is residual exposure to the experience they had while they were temporarily on the other side. This provides them with a different perception of life and death. They now understand what happens to our souls once we transition to the other side, and they can no longer tune it out. This can often be overwhelming, and many people say it takes many years to readjust to human life. They have been closer to heaven than most and almost go through a period of readjustment, bringing their new spiritual life into a life they once knew.

Some people have simply had experiences all of their life, with no rhyme or reason as to why they have always had this connection. Others have had no experiences at all, but they have a strong pull toward connecting to spirit on the other side. Regardless of how you come into your abilities or why you have been drawn to develop them, trust that there is a reason and purpose driving the call to explore and embrace your gifts.

Chapter One Exercise

Many people are interested in developing their mediumship or psychic abilities, but also feel they may be overreaching. They feel they don't have the gift, that it is outside of themselves.

What has drawn *you* personally to read this book?

Reflect on your calling and interests. Using a journal or the following pages, write down all of the psychic or mediumistic experiences you have had. Remember times when you've picked up things about other people you may have dismissed as just synchronistic. Recall any experiences you have had in sensing spirit in any way. Write them all down and reflect on them. I think you will see that you are here for a reason. We all have some level of psychic or mediumship abilities even before fine-tuning them.

CHAPTER TWO

Intuition vs. Empath vs. Psychic vs. Mediumship

*"One of our greatest gifts is our intuition. It is our sixth sense we all have.
We just need to learn to tap into and trust it."*
~ Donna Karen

There are varying degrees of psychic and mediumship abilities. We all have experiences that fit into a few of the categories of psychic abilities. This distinction leads us to learn and explain more about when experiences are happening versus chalking them up to coincidences. We can learn how our experiences start and how deeply we can develop our intuition, empath, psychic, and mediumship skills. Remember, the more you tune in to anything in life, the more it grows. Take note of all the experiences you have had and start looking at them as actually receiving and perceiving information.

Intuition is something we all have. It's our internal guidance system, which helps us make aligned or beneficial decisions for ourselves. This is the nudge, or "gut feeling" people get. Intuition is different from judgment or worry. It is usually one of the first thoughts or feelings you have when making a decision or encountering someone.

Our human brains tend to overthink things and cause stress or repetitive thoughts. Stress keeps you awake at night. Intuition, on the other hand, comes from your "gut brain." It is a gentle knowing that doesn't cause fear, stress, or worry. It is a soft nudge trying to help guide you. Intuition is the feeling you get when driving down a road, and suddenly you know you should take a different way home, but you ignore it, only to find out that the traffic is stopped on your regular route due to a car accident. If only you had listened to your intuition, you would have saved the forty-five minutes you now are spending waiting in traffic. Intuition is the feeling you get when encountering someone and just *knowing* that you are going to connect, or that they are someone you want nothing to do with.

Intuition aids us in making decisions that are intended to help us in any given situation. Intuition is reflexive and immediate; it is *not* the thoughts that keep you up all night worrying or that create fear. If you are ever uncertain if a thought or feeling is your intuition or not, take a moment to contemplate whether this gut feeling would help you in any way, or if it would guide you to what you are trying to achieve, get you where you are going, or protect you in some way. Try following this feeling to see if it helps you in any way. If it does, it was your intuition; if not, it was more than likely just a fearful thought.

Trusting is the first step in growing your intuition. It should always come as a gentle or persistent nudge and have a positive outcome for you. Sometimes, we pick up on things that let us know something *less than positive* may happen. Know that this is simply your intuition helping you to make a safer decision or avoid a negative situation that might occur if you choose not to do anything about the gentle nudge. This still should be a gentle nudge and not a fear-based repetitive thought. The two *feel* very different.

Empaths are people who tend to want to help other people. Being empathic is really understanding how someone else is feeling or what they are going through. Empathy is a bridge between intuition and psychic abilities. Many empaths pick up on the feelings of others, and sometimes, knowingly or unknowingly, they feel in their bodies what others are experiencing. You know those videos on television with the funny bloopers of people getting injured? To empaths, these videos aren't funny at all. It's not that what is happening isn't humorous, it's simply that empaths actually pick up on what the injured person is feeling. It quite literally hurts them too. It is the same for an empath if someone is crying or laughing. Most people have this experience from time to time, especially with people close to us, as we are both spirit and human. Remember, we are connected to everything: people, places, and things. However, true empaths will have it happen all the time and even in encounters with strangers. It can be overwhelming.

While having a response to others' emotions is natural and part of being human, empaths feel it more than the average person. If someone is sick, they may feel the same as the person just from being around them, or they may develop similar symptoms. It can be hard for empaths to be around sad or angry people for long periods of time because of the tendency to pick up on their feelings. Because empaths tend to want to help people and lift them up so that "everyone feels better," it can be draining for their energy and often will make them feel tired. In these situations, it is healthier for an empath to avoid people whose discomfort or pain cannot be separated from the empath's experience. Empaths usually learn over time to be choosy about who they are around, to better manage their own emotions and feelings.

Psychic ability is when one is able to tune into the energy of other people, places, and things around them. This usually starts with the psychic person not knowing whether what they are feeling is their own or not. Like the empath's experience, this can be overwhelming. Many times, psychic experiences are similar to empathic experiences. However, beyond feeling a mood, emotion, or physical pain, the psychic experiences *feeling, seeing,* and *knowing* detailed information. Psychically picking up information about others can make people feel as if they have anxiety, simply due to the information overload to the nervous system that can happen when they feel everyone else's feelings.

As an example, I used to work with end-stage disease patients. After my patients received their treatments, they would feel exhausted and need a nap. It is no coincidence that for the first several years, I too would go home exhausted and need a nap. I am naturally a helper and was quite literally taking on my patients' energy without even knowing it was exhausting me. I share these experiences and what may be happening prior to you taking charge of your abilities so you know you can gain control of them. You don't have to let them control you, and you don't have to feel overwhelmed or exhausted once you set the right practices in place.

Psychic information can be received by hearing, seeing, feeling, or a deep sense of knowing. Each person's abilities are unique and specific to them. In general, psychics have the ability to tune in to someone's past, present, or future, to receive information for the person or place they are reading. Often, the person being read will know most of the information the psychic is bringing forth, but will gain some insight, answers, and solutions they may have been unaware of. This revelation helps the recipient put the puzzle pieces together to understand certain things in life more clearly. Insight and clarity regarding choices to be made are usually why someone will seek out a psychic reading. Remember, psychics can also read the energy of a room, location, item, or event.

Mediumship is the ability to connect and communicate with the spirit world. Mediums are always psychic and have the ability to connect to living people's energy as well, but not all psychics tune in to spirit or have mediumship abilities. Mediums receive information the same way as psychics: hearing words and phrases, seeing people and images, or feeling information related to the passing of the spirit. They may "smell" scents, such as cigars, perfumes, or baked pies, and can "taste" as well. This is the same as being psychic but tuning in to a different energy beyond the physical plane. All mediums receive information differently. Most have a combination of "clair" senses (extrasensory abilities). (More on this in later chapters.)

During a reading, the medium or psychic combines all the information they receive through their extrasensory abilities and turns it into communication for the person who wants to connect to their loved one in spirit or gain insight and answers around specific situations. The goal of mediumship is to provide validating evidence, so the person receiving the reading knows that, in fact, their loved one in spirit is safe and at peace on the other side. Many people report being able to live a fuller life knowing that there is continuity of life and that our souls live on after leaving the physical world. Knowing their loved ones haven't truly left them and that they will meet up again when they too cross over one day is beyond comforting.

Giving readings can be difficult at times, especially when dealing with grief, but it can be healing and fulfilling for ourselves as well. Psychics and mediums benefit from the joy and healing they bring to people's lives through clarity, peace, and hope for the future.

Now that you are aware of the types of abilities, we are going to get into some practical things you can do to start tapping further into yours.

Chapter Two Exercise

Let's review what we've learned in this chapter:

- Intuition is our gut feeling; we all have this ability.
- Empathy is the ability to feel what others are feeling.
- Psychic abilities include perceiving knowledge from people, places, and things.
- Mediumship abilities include receiving knowledge from those no longer in the physical world.

Considering this and looking back at the events you captured in the Chapter One exercise; reflect on the kind of experiences you've had. Intuition, empathic, psychic, or mediumship? Use the next few pages to capture your thoughts on these and include details such as the approximate time and date, your location, and any other details around when these happened.

CHAPTER THREE

Meditation and Grounding

*"The goal of meditation isn't to control your thoughts, it's to stop letting
them control you."*
~ Dan Millman

S lowing our overactive mind is the first step in making space to receive
new information through our gifts. When we are busy rushing around
from one thing to the next and bogged down mentally from stress, we
create a barrier to connecting to and receiving information. This is why
meditation is beneficial.

Meditation is a great way to connect with spirit. Although some
mediums do not choose to meditate, and it isn't required to connect,
it helps to slow your mind and thoughts down so you can focus on
developing your abilities, especially in the beginning. When you quiet
your mind, you create an internal state of calm and peace. When
connecting to spirit, that internal peace and calm is important, because
it offers a blank slate for spirit to start communicating.

Meditation helps raise your vibrational energy, which can also help
with connection. Mediums here in the physical world are essentially dense
physical energy. Spirit is of a high vibration, with no physical body. Spirit
has to slow down or lower their vibration, while we need to increase or
raise ours. Meditation helps to remove a lot of the mental clutter and

stress from our daily lives, which allows for this higher-vibrational state, so it can be a great addition to your practice.

Participating in regular meditation allows for your calmer state of being to be more receptive and open to any information coming in from the outside. You then can gradually learn how communication works, and you can begin to identify which "clairs" you receive information through. This will help you to better understand spirit communication, so you can start receiving information in a non-meditative state.

Most mediums find that their abilities grow after regular meditation. They learn how to intentionally tune in to the energetic world and become more aware of everything surrounding us that they hadn't paid much attention to previously, which is important while developing your abilities. Many people find that regular meditation also brings a sense of calm to their outer world. Developing a regular practice of meditation can help you start to enjoy feeling more peace in our fast-paced world. During meditation, we begin to understand how much we can control the things we experience and how much they impact our daily lives. Being more mindful and bringing more peace into our lives allows for the shedding of negative thought patterns we may not have even been aware of previously. Meditation brings the understanding that our thoughts impact our overall well-being. Through regular practice, many people experience an increase in their overall health and relief from many health conditions.

There are many types of meditation. Guided meditations are a great way to start for beginners. It can be challenging the first few times you sit down to meditate because of your mind's natural tendency to engage with the internal mental chatter of the day's stresses. This is completely normal and to be expected. Your mind will slow down with practice. Many people find it easier to create a routine and connect daily. It helps if you set the intention to connect to spirit when you meditate, because they then know when to show up.

When I first began, I meditated prior to giving readings, as it helped me to clear my mind from the day. I also found that I would start connecting to my sitter's loved ones in spirit (they were stepping in early and were ready for me to read for my sitter), so I would take that information with me and add it to the information I got *during* their reading. Sometimes information coming in from spirit will be obvious, and other times it may be quite subtle. Pay attention to everything that comes in that doesn't relate to you and what you are doing. Little things that come in that don't seem important to *you* as the reader may be *very* impactful to the person you are reading for, so be sure to pass it on, no matter how silly it may seem. If you do encounter details during meditation that may seem irrelevant at the time, I recommend writing it down, so you don't forget. You too will probably find that information will come through prior to a reading and during meditation for your next appointment. Often once you start reading, you will become preoccupied and forget about the information, so having it written down somewhere will help. Your sitter might mention specific things about their loved ones during the reading, and you will realize it was the exact information that had come to you *prior* to connecting. With practice, you will learn how and when information starts coming in and begin to retain everything better.

Being psychic or a medium can feel overwhelming, due to the energy you pick up from others. Meditation can be a good way for you to tune in to what is going on with you that might need more attention. It may provide insight into the need to disconnect from distractions and tune in to what *you* need in the moment. When you have or are developing any abilities, whether psychic abilities or mediumship, it is important to take time to tune in to what is going on internally with you. Meditation is a great way to calm down the external energies of stress and everyday life to allow that to happen.

Your brain experiences many different types of brain waves, which naturally put you in a different state of reception and perception. I am a nurse as well, so I love understanding how and why things happen. I love teaching people about the different levels of brain waves that mediums experience. These patterns have been studied by many physicians to see how mediums' brains work differently. Brain waves, in order from alertness to the sleep state, are as follows: gamma, beta, alpha, theta, and delta. Delta is only really reached during deep sleep. It is a completely unconscious state. The others represent different states of alert but altered consciousness.

Most people function in the gamma and beta wave state throughout the waking day. It has been demonstrated that when mediums are connected to electrodes during readings, their brains experience the alpha and theta wave states, yet remain fully functional and alert, while the average person's brain will only reach the alpha and theta wave state during a long or deep meditation or light sleep. When we talk about raising our vibration to connect to spirit, we are quite literally doing that with our consciousness when we connect. Now you see just how beneficial meditation can be!

During meditation, especially if you try to do it for an extended period of time (fifteen or more minutes), you may sometimes feel a little bit disconnected upon returning from the meditation. That is because you go from experiencing theta or alpha brain waves back to a more awakened delta or beta state. Over time, you will see that you can reach an altered brain wave state without effort or meditation, if you choose. It will become second nature, because your brain has adapted.

Meditation can be done just about anywhere. You can meditate sitting down with your legs crossed, sitting in a chair with your feet on the floor, lying down, walking, or even while doing a repetitive task, like washing the dishes. Meditation is simply the awareness that you are disconnecting from your daily life, detaching from your thoughts, and allowing for the relaxation of your mind. I always find that wearing comfortable clothes helps, but anything will do if you are able to relax. It is all about the intention you set.

It is not uncommon for people to be disconnected from their authentic wants and needs in life. Society and outside pressures and expectations frame what many people want to accomplish in life. Expectations from school, parents, peers, and society's standards for success drive many people. Most of us get caught up in this at one point or another, trying to mold ourselves to everyone else's expectations. But until you slow down and tune in to your own needs, you can never be truly happy—not for the long term, anyway. Seeking love, validation, and accomplishments externally may temporarily fulfill you, but until you can fill it from within first and foremost, you will most definitely have some internal or external conflicts in life.

I found myself in this position, always feeling like I needed to go back to school to climb the ladder. I was more than halfway through nurse practitioner school before I decided I could no longer live the crazy busy life, nor did I want to. I was evading the peace I truly wanted. I was going back to school because I was missing something in my life that I thought would be fulfilled by advancing my career. It wasn't until I was halfway through that I realized it wasn't another degree that I was missing; it was my abilities that I had always wanted to bring to light. I wanted to express them, and this part of me that I had always shut down for the sake of others. I finally had enough. I had always been connected to spirit and was interested in everything metaphysical, so I made the change to living my authentic life versus one that led to more *external* accomplishments.

Remember that we are both human *and* spirit, and unless you honor both, something in your life will be out of balance. When you focus too much on the human aspect of things, like relationships, work, achievements, and family, you will eventually find that they move on to other areas in their own lives, leaving a bit of a hole in yours. You can temporarily fill this void, but you will always find yourself returning to needing more self-fulfillment.

I can say that being a medium and helping people to see that our souls live on, that we are so much more than just our humanness, is my biggest passion outside of my family, and I have never been happier waking up and living life as I was meant to. Helping others to find their passions and remember the bigger picture is part of that.

Remember to take the time to slow down and find the things that bring *you* joy in life, and then do them. Meditation is just one way to connect with your own internal wants and needs, and it can bring about many positive changes in your life.

Just as important as it is to meditate to help clear our minds, it is just as important to *ground*. Grounding is the intentional connection to the earth. Being empathic, you probably pick up on lots of energy around you throughout the day. Grounding helps you shed any of the connections you have made or energy you have picked up from others and return to your own energy.

One grounding practice I have found helpful and that I do most days is to envision roots from my feet, going down into the ground. As I visualize, I speak to the energy, stating that any energy that doesn't belong to me should return to the ground for healing. Then I visualize a white light coming down from heaven to cleanse and uplift my energy. If you are extra sensitive, envision a golden bubble of protection around you, acting as a shield. State that only love and light can enter, and that everything else will be returned to its source. Doing this daily will help you to feel better and set energetic boundaries, so you aren't picking up so much from your surroundings. This will help allow anything you have picked up throughout the day to leave you, so you are able to reconnect to your own energy space and feel lighter.

Getting outside with bare feet on the ground is a helpful way for empaths to cleanse their energy. There is a reason the saying came about to "step outside for a minute." Empath or not, we recenter by breathing in fresh air and connecting to our surroundings, things that don't carry emotions, just light and positive energy. It's an energetic reset. If you are ever feeling overwhelmed and picking up too much from others, I suggest doing this for several days in a row. I believe you will find that you start to feel better.

Another way of helping to cleanse your energy is to simply acknowledge that what you are picking up on is not your own. Your attention to the fact that you are feeling something that doesn't belong to you is usually enough to separate you from it. Asking whose energy you are sensing is another way of separating their energy from yours. You may see an image of someone or just get a feeling of who it belongs to. When you do this, your body and mind become aware of what is yours and what is not. You should feel the other person's energy leaving you if it's theirs, because your mind has now separated the two of you. Any way you choose to disconnect from other people's energy should be helpful.

The whole point to this is that you can learn to become aware of your energy versus their energy and separate the two to avoid feeling drained and overwhelmed by your abilities.

Meditation also brings your awareness to the fact that you are in charge of your own energy. Once you realize this, you have no reason to blame how you feel on others. You can tune in and tune out as much as you wish. You are in control of yourself, and that is important to remember.

If you find that you fall asleep during meditation, try a different position. Make yourself a little *less* comfortable. You can always try using meditation apps as well. Guided meditation is a great way to assist you and help stop the mental chatter that distracts you from being able to separate yourself from your daily stresses.

Remember that the biggest goal here is to slow down your mind so that you are able to start receiving the information. If your mind is cluttered, how would you know if what you are picking up on is yours, or if it is coming from outside of you? Slowing the mind allows you to relax, so you are better able to understand the differences. Slowing down the mind also helps to raise your vibration, so you can connect with spirit more easily.

Again, we are dense energy in the physical world, and spirit is of light and at a higher vibration in the nonphysical. I like to describe connecting psychically or mediumistically as meeting in the middle. We raise our vibration, and they lower theirs, so we can connect. Meditation is a great way to bridge the two worlds.

Chapter Three Exercise

Using the space provided in this book, write down your experience—both the struggles and the insights—each time you meditate. Find a place to meditate and get comfortable. This can be sitting or lying down. Just make sure you are feeling relaxed. Create a peaceful environment. Being in a room that is free of distractions makes meditation easiest. Some people like to have background music to tune out other noises. Many people ask for protection from God, spirit, or their guides when first starting out. I find that the more you tune in to connect, the more you will find that you don't need any protection at all. But do what suits your needs. If you ever have any doubt or fear, please know that you are the one in charge. You are in the physical, and they are not. You get to decide whom you will be connecting with. Spirit guides? Your loved ones? Other people's loved ones? Angels? They listen. They are waiting to connect. Trust in your abilities and know how powerful and in charge you really are. When you start to open up to spirit, you may find that several different energies try to connect. You can set the intention that only the spirit you are trying to connect with will step in. You will find that over time, you no longer need to set up boundaries or protection. This is because all spirits will eventually know what your expectations are.

- Define your intention. Speak it aloud. Do you want to connect to a loved one in spirit? Do want guidance on a certain topic? Do you just want to learn how to feel calm and more relaxed? State your goal for the meditation.

- Close your eyes. Take a deep breath and release it slowly.
- Breathe in for the count of four, hold your breath for the count of four, then exhale for the count of four. Continue to do this until you feel yourself starting to relax. After you do this four-four-four exercise ten times, you should start feeling tuned in. It is important to breathe from your stomach, not your chest, to make sure you are taking good, cleansing breaths. Being aware of your breathing pattern allows for your thoughts from the day to slowly melt away.
- Tune in to your body and notice any areas where you may be feeling stress. If you feel any areas of stress or tension, try actively breathing and visualizing your breath going into those areas to help with relaxation.
- If you find your mind running, you can envision whatever you are thinking about floating away in a balloon or down a river on a floating leaf, whatever works for you to help the thoughts go away. Try not to attach yourself to the thought but allow it to float away. This becomes easier with practice.
- Once you feel you have been able to calm your mind down and that your head is mostly clear, then ask spirit to step in and aid you in your connection to them. To start off, ask spirit a question and see what answer you get. Once you start to see that you do get answers, it will not only help you understand how you received the information (hearing, seeing, or feeling), but you will also start to see that spirit can absolutely communicate with you when you choose to tune in!
- You can spend as much time in this space as you need. Know that this can take time to develop, so don't be hard on yourself if it takes a few tries.
- When you are done, thank spirit for helping you learn. Start to feel the physical connections around you. Notice

the chair or bed you are sitting or lying on. Notice your feet on the floor (or wherever they are) and the sounds around you. When you are ready, open your eyes. Write down your experiences.

CHAPTER FOUR

Detoxing and Clearing

*"You will never follow your own inner voice until
you clean up the doubts in your mind."*
~ *Roy T. Bennett*

Similar to meditation and slowing our minds, it is important that we actively take a look at who we are, and how and why we show up the way we do. This is what I call "detoxing." You can have the most seemingly perfect life possible, but I can tell you, from all of the readings that I have given, that absolutely everyone has something to heal from or improve on. Detoxing is taking a look at some of the areas of your life that bog you down mentally, emotionally, and/or physically, and which prevent you from showing up as the better, more healed version of yourself. I cannot express how important this is when you are going to be taking on helping people who come to you with grief or trauma, or who are working on overcoming other things they are dealing with. Being a clearer channel not only for your own life, but for things that come up in mediumship and psychic readings will help you show up so much better for the people you will be connecting with.

When people are coming into their abilities, they may often find it beneficial to do some detoxing or healing prior to helping others. I leave this open to how you choose to interpret this, but it is important that when you are in a reading, you are able to see things from other perspectives, not just through your human eyes or the life that you have lived up until this point. We are all swayed by our own life experiences in how we perceive information, based on how we were raised or the situations we have lived and learned from. You see this in many people you encounter, who believe that how they think or what they know is the only way to see things. It is important to take a step back and understand that you will be helping people from all walks of life who have experienced so many things you may or may not have judgments about.

Detoxing may be required for many aspects of your life experiences. Detoxing does not mean changing the essence of who you are, because you are spirit and perfect in your own way. You are here for a reason, and it is important to remember that you do not need to change a thing about how or who you are. Rather, detoxing and removing things from your life that are not in your best interest helps the real you shine. This can be as simple as not spending so much time on social media or watching television. Detoxing may also include consciously identifying and relearning your responses to negative things you've experienced in life, which subconsciously affect the things you tell yourself. You may need detoxing from abuse you've been through, whether mental, emotional, or physical. It can also be something you learned when you were a child, or in a significant relationship, such as not being loveable or good enough. Your subconscious mind may take those things on as a fact, so you constantly place yourself in situations to make that "not good enough" a true statement. This truly is different for everyone. The point is that while it may have been helpful for you to grow and see your worth, it is baggage that you no longer need to hold onto if you consciously choose to let it go.

You will be giving readings and discussing things with people who can be quite sensitive. It is important to help the person see that we are all human and deserve great things in life. Beginning with doing that work for yourself is important for being able to give authentic readings that are not influenced by your past conditionings.

Many messages you receive will have to do with forgiveness, living more freely, or even having compassion for what we or spirit have been through. These messages ask us, as mediums, to look at things from a higher perspective, with true compassion and sensitivity. When you relate to your sitter through a similar situation, and you have truly detoxed from your own experiences and triggers, you are much more of a support and can be a better steward of the messages you receive.

Spirit wants us all to heal from the things that hold us back in life, so we can live more freely. All humans come from and return to spirit, and while many people in the world show up as or do things that we would regard as less than loving or kind, they too are spirit. Every soul is here learning a lesson, and it is not our job to judge, reframe, or skew information for the sitter based on what we have been through personally. All souls are made of love and return to love, no matter what experience they have here on Earth.

Forgiving is a big part of learning, both here and in spirit, and it is a key to helping free ourselves of unnecessary burdens. When we leave this Earth, during what is called a life review, we get to look back at the life we've lived, how we could have done better or what we could have done differently, and how our choices have impacted others.

The detox process begins for everyone at the moment it is supposed to happen, but I personally believe that developing our spiritual connection will stimulate this process, because you begin to tune into your soul self more often, which is naturally made of love.

Should you decide to develop and share your gifts, you are going to have to step out into the world and show up differently than what many people see as "normal." This takes courage. If you communicate with spirit, some people will harbor negative beliefs about you and have opinions about your beliefs. It will take standing in your own power and truly knowing self-love and your worth to withstand these influences.

Detoxing helps people look at the ways they have shown up previously to see what holds them back from allowing themselves to be authentically themselves. It shows you how important those attributes are in life, and how little others' opinions should affect you. Many mediums and psychics find what they help others heal can help themselves heal in some way as well. Many readers receive healing during their readings because the clarity and compassion spirit offers may help them to see things from a higher perspective and reveal ways that their own perceptions can still improve.

A word of caution: don't expect to one day wake up free of everything that has weighed you down. This is a learning process that happens over time. Remember, forgiveness is never about making anything right. It's about freeing yourself from having to feel those heavy feelings day in and day out.

Sometimes detoxing is linked to diet as well. I don't believe you have to eat differently to be a medium, but you may find that eating certain foods helps you feel better, which can help you to show up more fully in a reading. In general, the better food you take in, the better you feel in life.

If you don't choose social media as one of your detox goals, I highly suggest you take a look at how much time it takes away from you doing more impactful things in life. Many empaths are quite affected by negativity on social media or in the news. It's not always positive and can be a big-time energy vampire. But I know that it can be fun too. Who doesn't love watching a cute puppy video? Most of us have been in the same boat, intending to use social media for "a few minutes," and then finding ourselves on it for the better part of an afternoon, or logging back in every half hour to see new posts.

Before you get lost in social media or that TV show, consider all of your goals and ambitions and the time you could be spending with your children, spouse, pets, friends, or loved ones. Spending time with the ones we love is one of the most important things we can do in life. If you don't believe me, ask spirit, or wait until you start reading to hear some of the messages they give. I can promise you; it is never that they wish they'd spent more time watching other people's lives. Think of all the time you could instead be doing, working on, or achieving some of your biggest goals, like developing your intuitive abilities.

A big part of life is to live in love and joy, yet almost everyone must overcome some sort of challenge in life. For some people, their problems are obvious, such as abuse or neglect, addiction, a toxic relationship or parents not being present in their upbringing. But sometimes they are much more subtle, such as peers telling you you're ugly or not as good as someone else. Maybe it was a coach telling you that you needed to lose some weight to have a better chance at making the team. Even having a "perfect" childhood can be a lesson for some: growing up not knowing how to become independent and get a job, live alone, or have a relationship, because they have never had to reciprocate, giving something in return. Having a sweet, kind, and passive parent who never speaks up for themselves more than likely will teach you a lack of self-worth, as it is what you have become accustomed to, and that may be something you then have to work on. Get the picture? No one gets out of here without learning and overcoming obstacles in life.

The reason these things are significant is they can have an impact on us, as they are implanted in our subconscious mind. When we believe the things we've been told, they become part of the story we continually tell ourselves, and this can impact how we show up in the world. We then have to work at overcoming these beliefs.

All readings work differently, but I have found that many times in psychic readings, helping people to see why they are experiencing a series of events that keep coming up in life leads them to something that needs attention or detoxing. Awareness of these topics in our own lives can help with understanding, and our compassion can greatly improve how the sitter is then able to show up in the world differently.

Nothing is outside of your ability to cleanse or clear. If you have a connection, whether psychically or mediumistically, please know that you are in charge of the energies you pick up and carry around with you.

Cleansing or clearing can be as easy as mentally setting boundaries. Some feel they need other things, like crystals, sage, or palo santo. Others may try alternative energy healing, coaching, or counseling. When you realize you can cleanse your energy however you want to, and that you are truly in control, it becomes easier to set boundaries, so you no longer pick up as much junk from others—or if you do pick it up, you know how easy it can be to get rid of it.

Just a quick note on curses: they don't exist. No one human or event can affect or change your energy if you do not let it. You are in control of you. It is super important for you to know that, and for you to teach others the same. People can send you ill will or bad vibes, but you can just as easily not accept or surrender to them. You are in control of your thoughts, emotions, and energy—period.

Again, I want to impress on you how important it is to look at your own thoughts, beliefs, and actions to try to see where you can detox your emotional, mental, and physical spaces. All these things impact how you respond to and show up in the world. The clearer the channel you are for your readings, the more open you are to helping people through what they are dealing with in life, without any of your own judgments or hurts. As I mentioned, you do not need to fix everything at once. In fact, you can't, and this is not what detoxing is about. It is about seeing the things you have gone through with more compassion for yourself and others. Understanding how we may be living and showing up in ways that others have impressed on us rather than through our own higher perspectives. This process should be able to help you see how you have been affected by yourself or others and how important forgiveness, love, and understanding are.

Living in a cluttered home can create a scattered and anxious mind. Things that we take in visually have much more of an impact on the stress or peace we feel in our daily lives than we might realize. Your environment may be something that you have been wanting to detox from. Pick one thing for now. You can always come back and do this more after you see how much better you feel.

Most repeating negative patterns in life just need to be looked at and given some compassion, to see where they have come from. Remember that what you resist, persists. What you accept, transforms. By getting it all out and detoxing from these things, one at a time, you will start to see that they no longer hold the same power over you.

Chapter Four Exercise

Using the space provided in this book, go through these detox questions to take stock of what would most benefit and serve your mental space. Write it out and let it go. Writing something down is truly a great way of releasing thoughts and emotions for healing.

- Write out what things you have been through that are causing some sort of clutter in your life. Be specific and write out what the situation was, who it involved, how it impacted you, and how you have personally allowed it to continue to affect you.

- Is there anything you haven't given time to that needs some attention and love from you?
    - Do you have continual negative thought patterns about that thing that needs more time and attention?
    - Do you have any thoughts about your life experiences that have allowed this to continually show up for you?

- Sit for a minute or two and think of one thing you feel is holding you back in life.
    - Do you spend too much time on social media?
    - Do you spend a lot of your time doing things you later regret, when you truly wanted to be doing something else? Do you compare yourself to others far too often, always thinking that you should be or do better?

- Did someone say or do something to you that has really affected how you show up in the world?
- Did someone say something that left you doubting yourself or that caused you to start judging yourself too harshly?
- Would forgiving someone for something help free you?
- Are there any patterns you keep repeating due to unresolved feelings from your past?

CHAPTER FIVE

Clair Senses

"Pay attention to the feelings, hunches and intuitions that flood your life each day. If you do, you will see that premonitions are not rare, but a natural part of our lives."
~ Larry Dossey

"Clairs" are considered extrasensory abilities, also known as our sixth sense. We will explore each sense in detail in subsequent chapters, but first, let's review what they are. This brief introduction will help you understand the different abilities before you go deep.

In the physical world, we have five basic senses: hearing, seeing, feeling, smelling, and tasting. These same five senses are also used in the metaphysical world. The difference is that we add the prefix "clair" (which literally means "clear" or "light") to the same five basic senses we use in the physical world when they are stimulated within the metaphysical or nonphysical world. Each physical sense correlates with a nonphysical sense:

- Clairaudience ("clear/light hearing") is the ability to *hear* beyond the physical plane. For example, you may have "heard" children laughing, someone whispering in your ear, or your own name being called.
- Clairvoyance ("clear/light seeing") is the ability to *see* outside of the physical realm. Imagine a daydream but seeing flashes of

situations surrounding people or images of people no longer in the physical world.

- Clairsentience ("clear/light feeling") is the ability to *feel* energy and sensations beyond your physical body. These are often sensations in the body that mimic feelings, emotions, or physical pains of people that you are around or that are on the other side. (This is usually not painful and passes quickly.)
- Claircognizance ("clear/light knowing") does not correlate with a traditional physical sense but is one of the most common extrasensory abilities. This is when you suddenly *know* something about a person, place, or situation without even knowing how you know. We perceive subtle signs with our gut, and we can pick up that same information from beyond the natural world. When you simply pick up on information and know it to be true without having received any information about the subject previously, this is claircognizance.
- Clairgustance ("clear/light tasting") is the ability to literally *taste* things that you are not physically in contact with. For example, the taste of strong coffee, or tasting an apple pie.
- Clairalience ("clear/light smelling") is the ability to smell things that are not in the physical world. This often relates to loved ones on the other side, but I have had it happen psychically as well. Most commonly, it is the smell of cigarette smoke or perfume.

I will give an example of how your clair senses may appear to you. I remember one night several years ago that stands out to me. I woke up in the middle of the night and felt heat on my face as if I were sitting in front of a campfire, and I smelled the smell of what I thought was campfire smoke. I thought it strange, but I have had many experiences like this, so I wrote it off. Two days later, Colorado broke out in wildfires so bad that we had thick clouds of smoke that were raining ash. Forest fires smell the same as campfires (burning wood). I was simply picking up on the fact that we were going to have wildfires that would be affecting my area. Once you have experiences like this, you start to know when you are picking up on things that are about to happen.

It is important to note that in developing your clair senses, we all have particular clairs that are stronger than others. Most psychics and mediums have a blend of several. The more you use them, the more they grow, and you'll come to learn what each means and how they work.

Some people get caught up in trying to strengthen and develop their weaker clairs. Others may get caught up in wanting the abilities of others, rather than appreciating their own strengths. These distractions will slow your progression. Instead, I strongly encourage you to use your strongest clairs and simply practice the others, knowing they will come. When we focus on what we *don't* have, we only take away from our individual gifts. You have your abilities for a reason. Trust in them, knowing that your stronger abilities are likely purposeful, because spirit knows that's how you best receive information. The more you focus on your strengths, the better you will get at reading and interpreting information through all clairs!

All of our senses, both physical and clair, help you connect to the living psychically or to spirit and help you receive information that you can pass on to the person receiving your reading.

I want to emphasize again that every psychic and medium works differently. Every psychic and medium has an idea of how they want to receive information, but trust that as you work on your abilities, you will develop the ones that are strongest for you. Spirit is smart and will use the best method for you to receive information to help you with your readings. You can always work to develop other clairs but be confident that your natural strengths work best for you, and that is just perfect. In the following chapters, I will go deeper into the clair senses and explain more about each, so you know how they work and how you can develop them.

Chapter Five Exercise

Using the space provided in the book, revisit your responses to the exercises so far. Then consider and write your responses to the following questions about your own clair senses:

1. Reflect on how you feel you have picked up information from others or those in spirit.
   - Have you heard, seen, felt, knew things about, or smelled a loved one in spirit?
   - If so, describe that experience and what senses were activated.
2. Think about all the ways you have tuned in with your senses.
   - What is your strongest sense?
   - How might you want to grow or connect to other clair senses?

CHAPTER SIX

Clairaudience

"Clairaudience is one way in which our higher self, spirit guides, angels, and loved ones in heaven communicate with us."
~ Jessica Lee

Clairaudience means being able to hear messages beyond the normal range of hearing. One sign that you may be clairaudient is if you easily get overwhelmed with lots of loud noises or music. During readings, clairaudient messages tend to "drop in." You *know* they are external. It is hard to explain to someone that has never experienced this, but it is different than your internal voice—the one that likes to think through everything. When you are thinking to yourself, your voice tends to have its own undertone. When it comes from spirit, it comes from out of nowhere and doesn't have anything to do with your train of thought or what you are thinking about. For example, you are at a reading, talking to the sitter, and giving your introduction, but you keep having the word "Mom" pop in. This is simply the mom in spirit starting to step in to let you know she is present and will be coming in during your reading to connect with the sitter.

Clairaudience is hearing messages from the spirit world. Psychics can intuitively hear messages this way as well. Common information that comes through clairaudiently are the identification of the spirit, names, personality traits, words or phrases that would have been important, jobs, hobbies, and music they would have listened to, or they may talk about memories. These can come through in the form of individual words or full sentences.

Songs are frequently heard by clairaudient psychics and mediums as well. There may be certain pieces of a song that come through as a way to express more information at one time. As an example, in a reading, I have heard the theme song of the *Happy Days* television show, so I knew the person watched *Happy Days* and that it was more than likely something they enjoyed. Sure enough, the girl I was reading for said that was her grandmother's favorite television show, and they used to watch it together when she would go and stay with her. It's the same for the show *Family Matters*: I have heard the song "Fishin' in the Dark," and because that was the phrase that kept coming to me, I knew the spirit I was connecting with loved fishing in the dark literally in the early morning hours. The daughter laughed and confirmed that her dad was a huge fisherman and only ever fished in the early mornings before the sun came up. She said he swore that was the only time of day to catch fish. Separately, I have heard songs by The Beatles and techno dance music in other readings and knew this was just the type of music the spirit would have listened to, because no specific phrases were repeated. It's always specific to the soul coming through.

I ask spirit to bring me things directly, not just in symbols, so less "figuring out" is involved. On occasion, I have felt the impulse to tune in to classic rock music, or felt like dancing, and I know that if I am heading into a reading, it is spirit that is prompting me to tune in to that specific genre of music.

You just have to pay attention. Our loved ones truly connect to and lead us in so many more ways than we pick up on. It takes tuning your focus to the gentle nudges, and you will see that they are much more prevalent than you may have previously recognized.

There are two types of clairaudience. One is hearing an external voice or a disembodied voice. The second is through the voice of your own thoughts. Disembodied voices are a bit less common, as it takes a lot more energy for spirit to be heard through the physical hearing sense. It is a message that comes from *outside* of you and doesn't match anything you're thinking about. When this happens, you can usually distinguish what the voice is saying, and it can be a bit startling, as there may be no one else in the room with you.

The second is internal, and over time, you can distinguish spirit from yourself. The message drops in and usually in some way has to do with the description of a spirit. Mediums may hear accents or get words in other languages, helping us know that the spirit is from a certain culture. I once heard a man speaking a language that I didn't recognize. It most definitely wasn't a language I had heard in my waking life up until then. I truly wasn't sure what language I was even hearing, but passed it on to the sitter, and she laughed and said her father spoke Greek. That was neat!

I want to add that hearing spirit can come with a negative perception. As I mentioned before, hearing names and descriptions of people is much different than what many people might label as "crazy." No doubt, many mediums go through an experience of shedding society's perceptions that they are "different."

Let me emphasize that spirit never will direct you to do anything that is not positive in nature. If you do ever hear anything negative, please know that this is *not* spirit, but either a link with a mental illness or negative aspects of *your* mind related to fear. If this is the case, I recommend counseling or making an appointment with a physician to figure out the cause. If you are here and learning about mediumship, it's safe to assume you hear or will hear information linked with actual spirit.

Heading into this chapter exercise, consider that sound is so much bigger than the basic sounds you choose to tune in to daily. Dogs can hear sounds up a quarter of a mile away. We train ourselves to tune in to the sounds that are directly around us because honestly, tuning in to anything more can be quite distracting and unnecessary. However, that does not mean we *can't* hear more. Think about the last time you were having a conversation with someone only to find out they didn't hear a thing you said. They were busy with their own mental chatter, or focusing on something else. We teach ourselves to do this because too many sounds can be overwhelming. We are human and spirit made of energy, and therefore, we can tune in to so much more than we have trained ourselves to believe is possible. You just have to open your mind to it.

Chapter Six Exercise

The following exercise will help you to pay attention to even the most subtle sounds. You will *think* of different sounds, and *how* they sound, in as much detail as possible. For instance, if you are hearing a train pass by, listen to the train's wheels on the tracks, the whistle of the horn, the excitement of children as the train passes by.

Think of children in a classroom: what the teacher might be saying to the children, what the children may be saying to one another or laughing about, the sound of pencils dropping to the floor. Doing this exercise in a quiet room will be helpful.

You can also grow your clairaudience abilities by simply listening to music.

Using the space provided in the book, capture what you heard and experienced after doing the following exercises. You should start to subtly pick up on sound that you have previously tuned out. Spirit also knows that you are working on trying to hear them. When you take a step towards them, they do so in return.

1. Hear what it sounds like for a dog to walk on a hardwood floor, what the rain on your roof sounds like, or what wind chimes blowing in the wind sound like.
2. Listen to one song many different times, tuning in to a different element each time. Follow it through the whole song, no matter how soft, and tune out everything else. For example, the first time, listen only to the singer, the second time only to the drums, the third time only to the piano, etc. We are accustomed to listening to a song as a whole, rarely

to each different element, but they are there when you pay attention. You will hear so much more in doing this exercise. Keep practicing your ability to discern messages from noise. Write down what you heard and record your progress.

Exercise

CHAPTER SEVEN

Clairvoyance

"Always look beyond what you can see."
~ Mark Cooper

Clairvoyance is the ability to see things beyond our normal visual acuity. Some refer to this as seeing with your "third eye." Clairvoyance can show up in a couple of different ways. I will describe both, because I have experienced both. I personally believe that most people have some of this ability, but don't even recognize it or know they are tuning in to their clairvoyance.

We have been taught that we see certain things that are "normal," and we don't see others that are not. In my opinion, this can cause our perception of what we individually experience in life to be jaded by others. You are taught certain things early on in life, which tends to be when most people frame their understanding of what is okay, safe, and "normal," as well as all the things that are supposedly the opposite. This is also known as cultural conditioning.

One of the parts about this I find to be ironic is that America tends to be one of the only places in the world that doesn't accept connecting with the deceased as a normal or traditional practice and thinks it to be a bit taboo. In Mexico, there is a day dedicated to connecting to and celebrating the dead (the Day of the Dead, or *Día de los Muertos*). Many other South American cultures set up altars to pray and meditate to connect with their deceased loved ones. Other cultures meditate daily to connect to spirit while some create dance rituals to celebrate and become closer to spirit. Many native cultures believe one of the *purposes of life* is to connect to the greater spirit. In Europe, they have mediumship colleges and have established what modern-day evidential mediumship consists of. Almost fifty percent of adults in the US have had an experience with a loved one after their passing, and thirty percent have *seen* an apparition of a spirit. The list goes on and on.

Children tend to be the most receptive to spirit. They haven't yet been taught that seeing Grandma or a childhood friend who has passed isn't okay. It's not until we enter school that we start learning what ghosts are and that they only reside in stories and books. This is when moms start telling their children that their experiences are "make believe." All of this is taught, but there can, and will, be some undoing of this in life if you have the ability to connect to spirit. Our souls can't help but unlearn what isn't true to us, no matter how hard we might try.

We are all human, and there is a huge blessing in that. But we are spirit, so connecting to our loved ones who have crossed over is not only possible, but something that can help people live again. If our souls live on after death, what is there to fear in dying? What if getting a visit from our deceased Mom who just happened to be our best friend helped us to *live* and feel more peace? Not only for the time we have left on earth, but so we didn't have to fear death so much, knowing they are still very much alive. What if this *is* normal?

Spirit can be seen through clairvoyance in two ways. The first way is external—actual physical apparitions that you see *outside of your body*. Most external spirit experiences happen in one of two ways. The first is when the spirit takes on a more physical form. Most people report seeing a gray, translucent figure in which you can still see all the details of the spirit in a prominent form. This is what some people call seeing a "ghost." Most spirits tend to either appear as you last saw them toward the end of their life, or how they looked when they felt happiest in life, when they were feeling their best. Regardless, they are recognizable.

One of the most memorable clairvoyant experiences I had related to my nursing career. One Friday afternoon, I was at home and went to lie down on my couch to take a nap, when I felt this strange feeling that I needed to open my eyes. I sensed something. I looked down at the end of my couch and saw one of my patients standing there. I blinked several times to make sure this wasn't my imagination and looked up again to see him still standing there, just looking at me, at peace, but making his presence known. He had the same grayish translucent appearance as the spirit who'd visited my son, but this time with even more details—so much so that he almost seemed to be a solid figure. I could see his eyes, the clothes he was wearing, and his slight grin. I looked at the clock. It was 2:18 p.m. This patient was also my friend. If you've ever taken care of the same patients' day in and day out, you know it's hard to not make connections with them. They become family. He knew I could see him, and he was making his presence known. He was helping me connect the dots of all my experiences and letting me know that what I had seen and experienced was in fact real, and that all my houses hadn't been haunted. I had the ability to connect to the spirit world.

Of course, I went to work Monday morning and waited for someone to tell me this patient had passed away. No one mentioned anything, so I called his spouse to check in on him and got confirmation that he had, in fact, passed away … on Friday, at almost the same exact time I'd received a visit from him in my living room. He was just stopping by to say hi on his way out.

The other way that spirits are seen outside of the body is much less common. Several mediums have said that they see spirit in "human form." In this form, the spirit appears as solid as the object sitting next to you, and you can have meaningful and impactful conversations and exchanges with them. Some report communicating with these spirits who seem to be human, only to turn around and find no one present. They may be experienced passing in a hallway, in elevators, on trains, or sitting in a nearby chair. I have never had one of these experiences myself but have heard them explained. From what I gather, they seem to be solid in form, but then just evaporate into thin air, making the person question if the exchange ever happened, even when the conversation was very impactful and life changing. Almost like a visit from an angel.

Outside of the external, physical form, the second and most common way that spirits are seen is with the third eye. This is what most psychics and mediums refer to as clairvoyance. The best way to describe seeing spirit this way is that they usually have more color, are translucent, and look almost the same as if you were in a daydream. Imagine looking at a white wall and envisioning your mom or your dog, Max. You can clearly see the image of them, but in your head, in a spatial way. This is how clairvoyance works for mediums.

Pets come through quite often, as people find them to be a huge source of healing and unconditional love. When you give a reading and tell the sitter they have a horse in spirit, and you can describe the details of what it looked like, how can anyone argue with that, given that so few people ever even *own* a horse? It's hard to dispute when you can give details of items passed down, which no one would ever be able to just guess at or know about. Or when you can describe unique features the spirit had in life and that few knew about. These details provide validation that while in the reading state, we are able to connect to spirit and get evidence. Spirit does, in fact, stay around us, wanting to provide healing messages and let us know they are still here, even though not everyone may see them in the same way. We just have to make the choice to tune in.

Many mediums who have strong clairvoyance like to describe the spirit as they are seen. "Spirit artists" are able to draw the spirit in detail, on paper, as the medium is seeing them. This helps the sitter compare the drawing to a picture, portrait, or memory, validating that their loved one was in fact present for the reading.

Clairvoyance can also be used to see other aspects of the spirit's life. Pictures, items that would have been important to the person, adventures that were taken, details about the house they lived in, specific situations that happened around their passing, and current events in the sitter's life are all things that spirit may show the medium. I have even seen spirit write out their name for validation!

Mediums and psychics can use "remote viewing" too. Remote viewing is when the psychic or medium can tune in and see objects, people, and places from another location that is separated by a distance. You can use remote viewing to help tune in and get more information from spirit about their lives. This was also used by the US military created a program called 'Star Gate" to spy on other countries for decades. They would assign a coded number to a certain location or target. Everyone would tune in to this number and start sharing what they were picking up about this target. They later renamed the project and chose not to share it with the public, to avoid bias about the information that was received and used. I highly suggest trying this with a group of friends. I think you'll find that most people have this unknown ability to tune in to much more than they thought they did.

One way to describe the brain space used for clairvoyance is to think of a time when you were driving from point A to B, and you were startled to realize you were halfway to your destination and didn't remember getting there. You'd been zoning out and thinking of your day or daydreaming about another situation, but still very cognizant and driving safely. I truly believe daydreams are just our intuition's way of speaking to us, to let us know we are meant for more.

Chapter Seven Exercise

The purpose of this exercise is to begin to understand and know when information is coming in during a reading by practicing seeing images through your third eye. I suggest looking at a blank wall to help your mind clearly envision the objects. Each of these clairvoyant exercises will help you tune in to seeing beyond the physical. Using the space provided in this book, record what you see. How much detail is there?

1. Imagine a basket of fruit and see it in detail.

    - Choose an apple from the basket. Is it red or green? Are there any blemishes on the skin?
    - Choose an orange next and see all the details on its surface. Is it smooth or rough? Can you see any of the stem?
    - Choose a banana. Is it ripe? Does it have any brown spots on it?
    - Repeat this with seeing your favorite vacation spot and all of the details that you would pay attention to if you were actually there.

2. To develop remote viewing, imagine you're looking at an aerial view of a shopping mall.

    - Imagine standing above the mall and seeing the layout of each store.
    - Zoom into a shoe store.
        o How many clerks do you see?
        o How many shoppers are there?
        o If you are in the store and looking at a pair of shoes, which shoes are you looking at? Try to gather as much detail as possible.

CHAPTER EIGHT

Clairsentience

"Go where you feel most alive."
~ Author Unknown

Clairsentience is the ability to feel beyond our regular senses. For a medium, this shows up in the ability to connect to the spirit's health while they were living, feelings, and emotions.

Before reading, I can feel how spirit will be coming through. They may be strong, quiet, a jokester, sassy, sweet, joyful, or flirty. I quite literally start to feel their personality. I can tell if they may have dealt with mental health issues, such as depression or anxiety. Many mediums sense physical illnesses the spirit crossed over from or dealt with in life as well. Psychics may experience clairsentience when they pick up on similar information from the sitter as well.

I remind myself to pay attention to mannerisms I take on during readings. If I happen to be talking a mile a minute, I know the person was chatty. If I'm talking really loudly and excitedly, I know the spirit was more boisterous. If I talk with my hands, I know they did something similar. If I continually say phrases such as "Don't count your eggs before they hatch," or "Don't cry over spilled milk," I know these are phrases the sitter will remember the spirit saying. I may find myself tapping my toes or tapping my nails on the desk if the spirit was an impatient person. When this happens, I know to bring it up to the sitter as a characteristic their loved one would have carried as well. You may find yourself making funny hand gestures, being more comical, feeling more reserved, etc.

These are all things mediums should pay attention to when giving a reading. Many of these signs are subtle but bring additional and meaningful information to a reading about the sitter's loved one in spirit. These all help provide the sitter with validation that who you are connecting with is in fact their loved one.

I often find that I scribble out a cross on my reading notebook when I am picking up on the spirit having a religious background. Another frequent occurrence is when spirit comes in with music prior to a reading, as mentioned in an earlier chapter. Music can come through by means of clairsentience by making me want to sing or dance as well.

I remember one particular day that made a big impact on my understanding of just how smart spirit is. Sometimes, after a long day, spirit will bring uplifting information not only for their loved one, but for the medium as well. I was just finishing a shift at my nursing job that was particularly stressful. I had thought about canceling the reading I had scheduled that evening because energetically I was feeling drained. Then I felt a younger girl in spirit start to come through who was full of energy and showed me she loved singing and dancing. I quite literally started channeling her soul and felt the pull to dance, so I started dancing in my seat at work and found myself singing along with almost every song on the radio. She was doing this to help uplift and reenergize me, as I believe she knew her mom and grandma really needed the reading. I cannot count how many times I felt the need to reschedule a reading after having gone home from my old job, only to be uplifted by spirit and continue with the reading just for them to be some of the most impactful readings of my career thus far.

Spirit knows best, and you will see that pushing through harder days and continuing with the readings will help you to feel more connected and aligned—not only in terms of continuing to do what brings you joy, but in helping you see the bigger picture. I tend to find that doing mediumship readings helps lift my own energy up, and I feel more energetic afterward.

Chapter Eight Exercise

In developing clairsentience, you can tune in to your body and imagine where and how each cause of a spirit's passing may affect you. An example would be to feel in your head a possible injury or brain issue. The same goes for anything related to the heart, lungs, throat, kidneys, liver, spleen, bones, or something systemic. You know where you would feel this, so pay attention during your readings, especially in your body, to where you start to sense certain feelings. If you are not that familiar with anatomy, you can look at an image of the human body to figure out where all the organs are located, so you can better correlate that with feelings you have in your body during a reading.

In the following example, try to feel as much detail as you can, and you will shortly see that your ability to feel more will be amplified. Using your journal or the space provided in this book, record your experiences during this exercise.

1. Focus again on the fruit basket to study how each piece of fruit feels:
   - Is it smooth or waxy?
   - Are there dimples?
   - Are there bruises or overripe spots?
   - Is it hard or soft?

2. Imagine you are holding a set of keys in your hand:
   - How many keys do you feel on the keychain? By feeling the different keys, can you tell what door they belong to—house or car?
   - How many rings?
   - Do you have any separate key chains attached? How many? Are they smooth or rough?

Exercise

CHAPTER NINE

Claircognizance

"Always trust your gut. It knows what your head hasn't yet figured out."
~ Author Unknown

Claircognizance is the sense of simply *knowing* information. This knowing comes from the center of your stomach. Some people call it a "gut feeling." This is the information you know about certain individuals upon entering a room. This is what tells you to go left or right when you're lost. It's what led the caveman to eat the berries that would be nutritious and not the poisonous ones.

This sense is something we all have. It is an extension of our intuition. This is our built-in guidance system to help us through any given situation in life, to keep us safe, to give us a better outcome, or to help us get to a better place.

Claircognizance is often mistaken for a coincidence. I don't believe in coincidences. Examples of this might be when you are thinking about a certain person, and they just happen to call. Or when you are in the same room with someone, and you both start talking about the exact same thing at the exact same time. This is you tuning into each other's energy, and it's no coincidence. It is all about receiving and being receptive. Most of the time, when you are feeling relaxed, this is enough for you to receive information, whether you are aware of it or not. It can be quite subtle if you aren't paying attention, and can be quite loud if it is something *trying* to get your attention.

Claircognizance can come through in mediumship as well. Sometimes you aren't sure if the information you are receiving is from your blended clair senses working together, or if you are receiving information from spirit, just like you do from living people. Over time, with repetition, you will learn how to receive information, and in what way you will receive it, so you don't have to be tuned in to the subtle information quite as much. You'll get certain pieces of information coming through and just know what it means, making it easier to compile and pass it on. It takes practice.

Many of our extra senses have been tested through scientific studies, and while some things are not always explainable, we do know that positive energy creates more positive matter, and the same for negative. We know that when you speak to plants and feed them negative words, the plant will start to die. Plants grow faster when you speak nicely to them, just as humans tend to respond better to positive feedback. It's not the words themselves, but the energy that is being sent with them. It creates a better and more positive atmosphere. The human heart creates the largest electromagnetic field in the human body. We can literally measure its energetic field in hertz. Not only can it be seen with equipment, but we also know it can be felt.

The same goes for tuning in to energy. It is there, though you can't always see it, but it exists and has one of the biggest impacts on humans making decisions. The more you trust the information you are receiving, the more you will start to see it grow. It can be hard to explain how you know what you know; you just do. This information is just as important to relay as with any other clair sense.

Chapter Nine Exercise:

A great way to strengthen your knowing is to practice making predictions and testing yourself. All of these exercises, over time, will help improve your claircognizance, and you will see just how much you already do this without even thinking about it. More than likely, this is already happening to you, but you just write it off as a synchronicity and deny that you are actually picking up information prior to experiencing it in the physical realm.

Using the space provided in this book, write down some of your predictions and the results, as well as your thoughts about this exercise. For this first exercise, you will need a deck of cards.

1. With the deck shuffled and spread out with the cards face down, practice these exercises:
   - Before turning each card face up, tune in and see if you think it will be red or black and of what suit.
   - Place the cards you got right in one pile and the cards you got wrong in another pile.
2. Repeat this exercise often. You will see that the "right" pile will grow with practice. Practice the following on your daily commute:
   - Predict what color of car will be right next to your parking spot at work.
   - Predict details about the person next to you at the next stoplight.
   - Predict who your next call or text message will be from.
   - Predict whether your neighbor's car will be in the driveway when you get home.
   - What time will you pull into the driveway?

Exercise

CHAPTER TEN

Clairgustance and Clairalience

"The world is full of magical things,
patiently waiting for our senses to grow sharper."
~ *W. B. Yeats*

Clairgustance is the ability to *taste* things that you are not actually taking in. This can be the taste of apple pie, chocolate cake, chewing tobacco, a pipe, or blood. It could be anything that will help you to receive information for your reading in that way. I have tasted blood, which wasn't so pleasant. It was combined with a pain in the head, which told me the spirit I was connecting with had a head injury and some bleeding. Some mediums ask for only pleasant information. Spirit listens, so tell them what you are comfortable with. I think everyone enjoys receiving information in the form of the taste of cookies much more!

Clairalience is the ability to smell something outside of our basic senses. This can be anything, but the most common are perfume or cologne, cigarette smoke, baked goods, flowers, or anything that makes you think of a specific person or situation the second you smell it.

In my experiences, I have smelled pipe smoke so strongly that I could taste it, and the same for perfume. It was as though it were being sprayed at me. I have also seen a man's hand dirty with oil and could smell the motor oil and was able to convey that he was a mechanic through that.

For most mediums, these are not the strongest clair senses, because you can only receive certain information about the spirit in this way. They can bring us additional information in this way, but it isn't usually the primary way of receiving information, since it can be quite limited.

I have personally found that clairalience and clairgustance also tend to be a very personal way for us to connect to our own loved ones in spirit. I don't have these clairs come through in readings very often. I do, however, sense some of my own loved ones in this way. I know that when I have the smell of cigars come through, I am picking up on the presence of my or my husband's grandfather. I also know that the smell of coffee early in the morning (when I don't drink any coffee) is the presence of my grandmother. If I were to smell moth balls, I would think of my grandma as well. They don't sell moth balls anymore for several reasons, so it's not a smell that I would associate with anyone else. It takes me back to the moment that I smelled them in my childhood, opening the dresser drawers at my grandmother's home.

I also find that spirit may bring up that their loved one getting a reading has smelled certain scents, odors, or aromas in a room that were completely unexplained. This validates the presence of their loved ones for them. It is a very personal experience because our senses are tied to memory. You know the second you smell the scent who it is that is visiting you.

People who are more sensitive to smells here in the living and have psychic senses are more likely to have extra olfactory senses as well. I also feel this to be true for someone who relies heavily on their tasting sense. Foodies and people who can describe the apple taste in wine when everyone else is like, "Uh huh, yeah…"—those sensitive people are more likely to naturally have this gift as well. Remember that working on any sense will help grow it.

While most mediums will experience this from time to time, I find that even though you may be able to add a neat validation to your reading, like the scent of Cool Water cologne, you can't bring through as much information with this as you would with developing your other senses, so I suggest focusing a bit more on the others.

Chapter Ten Exercise

To develop these particular clairs, we will revisit that bowl of fruit and imagine what each fruit smells and tastes like. The more you use these senses, the more you will understand what to look for in your readings. To help prepare for this, imagine what a fresh-cut lemon smells like versus a strawberry. After completing this exercise, write down your reactions and thoughts in the space provided in the book.

1. Focus again on the fruit basket to study how each piece of fruit smells.
   - Does it smell sweet or sour?
   - Does it smell strong or subtle?
   - Does it smell ripe or fresh?
2. Now, focus on how each piece of fruit tastes.
   - Is it dry and bitter, or juicy and sweet?
   - How is the texture? Soft or crunchy, or something else?
   - What is the temperature of the fruit, and how does that affect the taste?
3. Next, try thinking of different types of smoke—tobacco, campfire, electrical fire. Notice how each scent varies and affects your other senses. Try this with baked goods, wine, and coffee too.

CHAPTER ELEVEN

Signs and Symbols

"Symbolism is the language of mysteries. By symbols men have ever sought to communicate to each other those thoughts which transcend the limitations of language."
~ Manly Hall

When I was beginning my journey into readings, I truly thought everything came through in symbols. While symbols do come through, it is important to know that you can ask for direct information just as easily as a symbol, which removes the need to interpret from your readings.

 In my opinion, there are going to be things like messages that need to come through in symbology, because sometimes certain pictures or words mean much more than what spirit can convey.

When I see someone praying, I know to mention to the sitter that spirit hears their prayers. Spirit may then combine that with a couple of specific words that were heard. I also see hands clapping from time to time, and that is to let my sitter know that their loved ones are cheering them on. Symbols are so specific to the person giving the reading.

Like I mentioned, I wouldn't spend a ton of time with symbols, as spirit can give you more direct information. However, sometimes, they are needed. I do have to mention that most mediums will come across a symbol in their career that they have no idea what it means. Try telling the sitter what you see first, but it may take many readings to actually figure it out. Ponder what that symbol has meant to you in your lifetime. You'll eventually figure it out. Remember, if you ever feel stuck and don't know what spirit or your intuition is trying to bring to you, you can ask for it in another way and see if that helps to figure it out.

If you ever want to get a specific piece of information, and you just don't seem to be getting it, you can work with spirit and assign symbols. An example would be every time you see a horseshoe print, that means a horse is present, and if you see a cat's paw print, maybe that means a cat is present. Spirit is always trying to help, so if you feel stuck, ask them to work with you on whatever it is you want to bring through more of in your readings. You'll be surprised at how much they will collaborate with you to help show their loved ones that they are present. I have noticed that sometimes mediums give a piece of information but are afraid to get more specific. The more detailed, the better. It only helps to confirm that you are truly connected to their loved ones. Don't be afraid to ask spirit questions or for more details. It's a two-way conversation. They will work with you in any area in which you wish to grow.

The whole reasoning behind symbology in readings is that information doesn't come through in "sentences" from spirit, or in a psychic reading. If it did, every reading would be extremely easy to convey, and that isn't always the case, especially in the beginning.

Some people like to call their symbols "spirit dictionaries." It truly is like learning a different language, and it takes time. The only way you are going to get confirmation that what you are getting is correct is by relaying it to the sitter. Once you relay that piece of information, it creates space for your brain to receive more to pass on.

When you want to learn more about certain topics, whether it be health, languages, geographic information, or physical traits, it is always helpful to study that topic. For instance, if you want to be able to share how the spirit passed, it would be helpful for you to learn, at least in general, where the main organs are. That way, when you are in a reading and feel a pain or pressure in your body, or physically see the organ, you know what the spirit is trying to relay.

The same goes for geographic information. Maybe you want to get better at relaying where the spirit was from, or where they lived during their life. When you know locations, you may hear the name of the state or town, or you may see it on a map, or you may just know. You also may feel pulled toward a certain area. Creating a larger framework of knowledge for spirit to pull from helps tremendously in readings. Our knowledge helps spirit be able to pull from our own frame of reference.

Over time, passing on the information you receive gets easier. When you hear, see, feel, or know the same thing over many readings, you then know what to say next time. In the beginning, you may be told by the sitter, "No," or "I don't understand." Try reframing what you are giving. If you see your mom, and the sitter says, "No, I don't have a mom in spirit," then ask if they know someone named Jan. They may say yes, and then you may see your mom every time you have a spirit coming through named Jan.

Maybe you see pearls and ask if they had pearls passed down to them, but they say no. Then ask them if they know what pearls might mean. Maybe their aunt's name was Pearl. It may sound confusing at first, but trust that what you are getting is real, and don't let a "no" scare you.

I know several mediums who really got torn down when they were told no, even to the point of stepping away from readings due to fear of hearing no. I can't tell you enough that if you are receiving a piece of information, it is for a reason. Spirit is a divine intelligence and is here to help you.

I have learned to trust spirit more than my sitter. If I give a piece of information, and the person says they don't understand, I always say, "If it comes up in a reading, it is meant to be passed on, so set it aside and think on it." The majority of the time, people have come back with an "ah-ha," saying they talked to their mom, and yes, their father who passed away when they were young did in fact collect cigar boxes. You will see that that happens frequently, and I personally think it is even more validating, because it is something the sitter wasn't even aware of, or it was uncommon knowledge, but very much part of who that father was in life.

I recommend writing down your symbols, whether it be a picture, word, or feeling. You will see that when you do and get validation from the sitter that a saluting soldier means that the spirit was in the military, your "dictionary" will grow. Over time, you won't need to keep track as often, because it will become part of your new language. It will become ingrained in you. You'll then have a *mental* dictionary to use and build upon.

Many mediums read how their teachers taught them to do it. It kind of depends on whether they teach you through symbols or receiving direct information. However you've learned, I wouldn't recommend *unlearning* and *relearning*. I would just try to build on the knowledge you have already.

When I started out on my mediumship development, I also kept track of my dreams, writing them down. I would then Google "dream meaning for [x]." Our subconscious minds are always trying to help us through what our dreams convey. When you look up what certain dreams mean, you may start to see that some of those symbols come through in your readings as well. This may be another helpful tool in your development.

Chapter Eleven Exercise

Keep your journal or this book at your bedside with a pen or pencil. Record any symbols you notice in your dreams or that seem to recur over the course of your day.

1. How (under what circumstances) in your dream did you encounter these symbols?
2. Reflect on what these symbols mean to you personally.
3. Reflect on what these symbols mean in the larger world.
4. Try to understand what your subconscious mind is trying to tell you.
5. Set the intention that, if you encounter that situation in life, spirit will bring it to you through remembering this dream or item (whatever it was that stood out to you in your dream), and trust that it will happen.

CHAPTER TWELVE

Colors and Auras

"Colors, like feathers, follow the changes of the emotions."
~ Pablo Picasso

Remember when I said that some of the information you are taught will be at least an aspect of what comes through in your readings? I took a class a couple of years ago on colors and auras, and now, in many of my readings since then, I start off my readings by discussing what colors I see in the "aura" around my sitter and what that means they are going through.

I have always been interested in Eastern culture, and chakras are something I find fascinating, since they are all energy centers associated with certain colors. Everything is energy. As you develop your psychic or mediumship skills, you will find that it is all about using your extra senses and tuning in to the unseen energy of the living, or of those who have passed on.

I am going to give an outline of what colors mean, based on chakras, but I encourage you to use your own frame of reference if you already have one developed. I always know that, when I see colors around the person I am reading, they have to do with the person's *personality*, but they help me to tune in to some things they are working on or trying to overcome. I sometimes just have a strong knowing that if I see a certain color, I'm able to tune in to exactly what it means for the person, since each color can speak to a power center and/or a challenge area. Let's look at colors I have seen in relation to chakras and what they tell me about the sitter—both good and challenging things they may currently be experiencing when I'm reading.

Red is the color of power and passion. It is the root chakra. Red is about grounding into the earth. When I see red around a person, I know they can be passionate, but probably need to be outside to reconnect to their own energy, or they find the outdoors healing. Red is about feeling stable and secure, so this often speaks of someone going through a situation where they feel unsafe or are acting out of safety. This often means they are being called to trust and step outside of their comfort zone, and they may need to put some attention or healing towards feeling more secure and grounded. People that tend to have energetic blocks in this area may also experience lower back and/or leg pain.

Orange is the color connected to the sacral chakra. It is the creative and emotional center and tells me whether the person is creative and loves crafting and the arts, or if they should be tuning in to their right brain more and doing more creative things with their energy. These people feel better when doing crafty or artsy projects, creating things with their hands and emotional space. This helps them feel more balanced. Life can be so busy. Work and stress (the logistical side of life) can take someone out of their right brain entirely. This color also relates to the sex organs and their sensuality, so this can speak to people over- or under-utilizing their sexuality as well. Often if something is feeling off in this area, there is an under-expression or an ability to tune in to how we feel. Many times, if there is a block in this area, people may experience an inability to express emotions, over exaggerated emotions, irregular or painful menstrual cycles, over or underactive sexual desires or impotence.

Yellow represents the solar plexus and speaks to a joyful, energetic personality. This is the power center and can speak to someone going through a situation that is taking their power away. This is all about self-worth, self-esteem, feeling worthy of being seen and heard, and being able to own true confidence. If I know someone is going through a difficult time with this chakra, I recommend positive affirmations, meditations to help tune in and release old thought patterns, and doing things that push them out of their comfort zone to help build confidence. People with long-standing energetic imbalances here may experience gut health and digestive issues.

Green is all about the heart chakra. When I see a darker green, it tells me that the sitter is going through some heart healing. If it is more of a light green, then they are healers in some way. These people often do something in the healthcare field or help people in their line of work. Dark green is all about healing the heart and speaks to the person going through grief or some type of healing. Often, grief and healing are intertwined. I personally feel the best helpers/healers in life are those who have been through a situation and lived the experience of the people they are helping. Experience is our greatest teacher, and life experiences give people empathy in a way that cannot be taught through traditional school/books/education. When imbalances occur in the heart area, people may experience heart palpitations or chest pains/pangs, and when they are worked up by an actual cardiologist, there is no known cause, and the person doesn't carry any underlying heart issues. Think back to a time when you were experiencing a great amount of sadness, heartbreak or grief. It's likely you had some unexplained heart pain or irregular heartbeats. Your heart feels all of the emotions that you do. So does the rest of your body.

Pink is also connected to the heart chakra, but it stands for love. For me, pink is a soft, loving energy and speaks to the person's soft or loving nature. They are big caretakers and help or give to others. Pink is also the color of self-love. When I see pink around someone, I know they are going through some type of lessons related to self-love. When people are always showing up for others, they tend to lose a part of themselves and forget how to truly show up for *themselves*, first and foremost. These people benefit greatly from turning inwards and really trying to show themselves the compassion and love that they give out so freely. This means truly looking at all of things they don't like about themselves—

any actions, parts of their bodies, self-judgment, or feelings that they aren't good enough in some way. These people are learning that all of those things they don't like or appreciate about themselves are truly what make them so great. I always recommend that these people take time for themselves and do several things a day that make them *feel* good. They can then better show up for others with a different type of energy—a more balanced energy, without harboring any type of resentment for putting their own needs off.

Blue is all about the throat chakra. This is for people who are in some kind of career that involves a lot of teaching, such as speaking or education. Teachers, for example, often present with teal blue. A darker color of blue means that the person is underutilizing their voice and needs to speak up about things in life, whether at work or at home. These people would benefit from clearing the emotions stuck in their throat area related to things on their heart and mind. They need to know that staying silent just to keep others happy dumbs down their own energy and self-worth. These people have probably been through a situation that has shut down their ability to speak up when they need to. They are usually feeling that if they do speak up, their opinions will be shut down. They may be overly afraid of feedback from others or not being good enough in some way. Energetic imbalances in this area may lead to people having to frequently clear their throats, get sore throats frequently, or have imbalances in their thyroid.

Purple, for me, represents psychic ability and is connected to the third eye chakra. When I see purple, I know this person has abilities. These people usually think they have these senses but may want confirmation that what they are experiencing is real. These abilities are usually not being used, or the person is unaware that the experiences they are having are due to them picking up information from others. I usually am given what their strongest senses are, so they can get some confirmation. I try to help them understand how they can separate their energy from what they are picking up on about other people. (This can be a big challenge in the beginning, when they are trying to understand or further develop their abilities.) Imbalances in the third eye may lead to headaches.

White speaks to the crown chakra for me. This is all about connection to spirit and people who have mediumship abilities. I may be shown this to help them see how they receive information from their loved ones, and to help them to understand that they are in control of their abilities. People who are closed off to their intuition, psychic abilities, and connection to spirit/higher self may experience anxiety, mistrust, fear, or phobias, as well as sleep issues, like frequent night terrors. (From all the readings I've done, I've found that many people are closed off in this area, due to fear of the unknown or fear of judgment from others.)

Gray, for me, is not connected to any chakra, but tells me that the person needs to do some thought or energetic decluttering. This color is usually related to mental blocks, self-doubt, or anything that would mentally make them feel bad. Gray in any given part of their body tells me that their energy is off, and the person may be experiencing physical health issues in that area. I always tell people to go to the doctor to get things looked at and evaluated if I sense a dark gray in their physical body. Dark gray or black not associated with the body tells me they need a detox around a situation or person in their life, and they may want to think about disconnecting from that person or situation before it starts to affect their energy even more than it already is.

Colors can be helpful in readings because they help you tune in to someone's energy. Often, people are aware of the things you bring up, but when you let them know it is manifesting in their energy, they are more apt to take positive steps toward trying to overcome that issue when you help them find the cause. Sometimes, it is just about being aware that *they* are the answer they are looking for, and they have had the key all along.

Some of these results can be instantaneous, while others take time. This is especially true when there is a limiting belief, or something that has been ingrained from their early years. But as I like to say, nothing is outside of anyone's ability to achieve. When you give colors meaning, and they come up in your readings, trust the message that needs to be passed on.

I have picked up things in readings leading me to refer people out to physicians or alternative health providers. Any time I feel that something might be off or worrisome, I tell people to go to the doctor to play it safe. I often find there to be a direct correlation between certain chakras and emotions that need to be released or addressed. Our mental and emotional space very much affect our physical and energetic body. Emotions, when left unexpressed, can get "trapped," if you will, and cause discord over time. These things arise in psychic readings to help people understand, or to point to things they would benefit from putting some attention on. Over time, emotions can build up if not expressed or dealt with, and if left unaddressed, they can make us sick, or even long-term lead to physical illness or disease.

I want to mention that this is just *my* interpretation of the colors that I see, based on what chakras they correlate with. If you are already doing some form of reading and/or see auras, and you have begun your own interpretation of what colors mean to you, then stick with that. I have noticed that many psychics and mediums have a similar but somewhat different view of what certain colors mean to them. You are the interpreter of your readings and will know best what the color stands for or means to you.

Chapter Twelve Exercise

For this exercise, you will need a volunteer. Explain to whoever you are working with that you are working on seeing auras. Sometimes people see actual auras, but a specific color may also just come to your mind, or you may hear a color. Remember, you receive information on how your soul and spirit know best.

1. Have your volunteer stand in front of a white wall or door.
2. Look at them for a minute or two and see if you start to see a soft color developing around their body.
3. Use the colors listed in this chapter as a reference, or you can draw from your own knowledge of what colors mean to you.
4. Describe your interpretation to the volunteer.
5. Ask them for feedback on what resonates.

Exercise

Part Two:
Putting It All Together

CHAPTER THIRTEEN

About the Reading

"The job of a medium is to be the bridge between heaven and earth,
to reunite loved ones, to bring them closer together
and create comfort and healing."
~ Martin Twycross

Putting together all the things previously mentioned in this book is the most important part of being a medium. You can passively learn all of the techniques, and develop your clairs, but until you sit in front of someone and connect to their loved ones, providing them with validating information, you will only be connecting to spirit, gathering information.

Being in front of a sitter helps you receive real-time feedback. This will help improve your understanding of the messages, signs, and symbols you're receiving. Only then will you understand if seeing a red rose means the name of the person coming through is Rose, or if there is a significance to an actual red rose. As I stated before, you can ask for direct information from spirit, so not as much interpretation is needed, but there will always be certain things that have to come through in symbology. The sooner you get in front of people, doing practice readings, the better.

When you begin doing readings, don't begin by giving an hour-long reading. I would begin with ten to fifteen minutes to start and increase your time as you are able. Connecting to spirit and doing readings takes a lot of your energy, especially in the beginning. I remember, early on, feeling tired after development classes, and again when I began giving longer readings. There were times that readings would go over the twenty-minute range and leave me feeling energetically drained. It didn't last too long, usually just for that evening, but there will be a time when you have to recover your energy when you start out. My normal energy levels would return the next day. The first time I gave a big group reading for over an hour, I had a headache that lasted for a couple of days. It takes a minute to figure out the give-and-take energy balance when starting out. I know now that I was tired because I was giving too much of my own energy, but it was something I had to figure out, and I know most mediums go through that learning phase. I've heard of mediums doing large group readings for several hours or doing too many large group events in a row, just to find that they get sick, and it takes days or weeks to recover. Only you know your energy. Listen to it, and you will be okay.

You will know what amount of time is good for you and how long is too long. You will know when you're ready to increase the time, because you will no longer feel energetically affected, and you're able to continually get information for the whole reading. Just know that you do not want to start out reading for an entire hour, though an hour is a good time to work up to. I offer thirty-minute and one-hour readings and reserve an hour and a half to two hours for larger group readings.

Many people think that after taking a weekend class, they're ready to start doing readings full-time. I highly recommend setting a goal of taking several development classes. There are many different teachers and types of readings. You will find some teachers that you learn a lot from, and others that may actually teach you how you *don't* want to be in your readings. Understanding what you are picking up on psychically versus mediumstically is also important. You should be able to bring through information that identifies what soul you are connecting to that gives the sitter evidence that you are connecting to their loved one, before you give them the message of what that soul is here to say. Learning true evidential psychic abilities and mediumship is the ethical thing to do, not only for your clients, but in representing all psychics and mediums.

Committing to your development is important, and learning is ongoing. Some teachers excel in one area, while others excel in another, but I suggest combining several different techniques and creating your own type of reading. I also suggest setting a goal of a hundred practice readings before you start doing them professionally.

There are many things mediums must learn before putting themselves out there. The first is that you have an ethical responsibility when doing readings. Always strive to only deliver what you are getting. We are the direct translators for spirit, so it is important to only deliver what you get in your reading and deliver it with compassion.

Always be honest and truthful. All mediums have, at one point or another, had a sitter who refused to accept that a certain spirit was coming through. I have come to trust spirit so much that I know, in those cases, that either I am mistranslating something if the sitter doesn't understand, or the sitter was so set on receiving a message from a *certain* person that they resist the one coming through.

There will also be sitters who don't *like* that a certain person is coming through, because of their relationship or challenges in life. Many times, spirit comes through to apologize for their behavior or wrongdoing, but the sitter may not always be ready for that apology. I feel it is usually the latter, with people not wanting to hear from someone they still hold ill feelings towards. If they aren't ready to hear a message, that is okay too. You can always ask that specific spirit to step aside. Trust me, on a soul level, they will understand.

Never allow any of these reactions to sway your confidence or make you change the information just to satisfy your sitter. If they aren't happy with the reading, simply return their money. I have one teacher who taught me that if the sitter doesn't understand what you are saying within the first fifteen minutes, simply ask them if they would like to reschedule to another date or refer them to another medium. You will intuitively know what to do.

Just as with anyone else in your life, you will occasionally find that another person's energy isn't a good fit for you energetically. I found this to be true more so during my development because I doubted myself and shut down the connection. When you are growing as a medium or psychic, you learn what works and what doesn't. As your confidence grows, you will see that your connections and readings improve. Your boundaries become stronger, and you can ask for spirit to bring you people who are good matches for you. It really works!

I also want to mention that the great majority of your readings should have a really good accuracy percentage, but it is important to remember that we are in communication with someone else: spirit. While the majority of the information is direct, and you will know what it means, sometimes you have to remember that any time you communicate with another spirit or person, things can be open to interpretation.

How often do you text or email someone and mean something one way, but the other person takes it differently? For example, say you text someone, *No thanks!* meaning, *No thanks, I've got it,* but the recipient of the text thinks you're being short with them, or rude, just because you used an exclamation point. It happens. People hold extremely high standards for psychics and mediums and think they should be one hundred percent right all of the time. While you probably should be close to it if you want to do this professionally, no one is perfect at any profession, and that's the truth. If we held others to the same standards in their professions and never allowed for an off day, they might give psychics a bit more of a break.

As with any communication, it is important to pass on everything you get, but know that sometimes, the sitter may not understand what you're saying. Remember that mediumship communication involves three parties, and the conversation is impacted by interpretation. I only mention this because it is important to remember that communication between three people is not *always* going to be relayed perfectly. It *can* be extremely accurate, but give yourself a break when needed, and know that communication can be misinterpreted. Don't give up, and if you get a no, try to present it in a different way. Strive for accuracy, not perfection. I had a teacher that said it's helpful to think that the *P* in "perfection" stands for poison!

These days, it can be hard for people to trust psychics and mediums because of how many frauds are out there trying to make a quick buck. It is important for us all to ethically represent mediumship with only truth and honesty. Doing anything else only helps the skeptics and will hurt your business in the end.

Some mediums caution about doing on-the-spot readings, meaning someone who did not seek you out to give them a reading. This means you step forward and start passing on information that you are getting about the person or their loved one in spirit, without them asking for it. I am neither for nor against this. It definitely takes some courage to deliver, because you never know if the person you're approaching is a believer in the afterlife or open to spirit messages, so it is important to identify yourself and what you do, then ask them if they are open to a message. This gives them the free will to say no and walk away, or to be open to it if they choose.

Development circles are everywhere. Development circles are places (online or in person) where mediums or psychics get together and do practice readings on one another. There is always one person or a teacher leading the group who usually teaches on a certain topic and then has the students practice that skill. These are great spaces for new mediums and psychics to practice, as everyone attending is a medium, and there is no judgment. You can get real-time feedback from other people who are also developing their skills. This is a great way to build your confidence and get those practice readings in.

Friends and family can be good, safe places to practice, but remember, the point of giving an evidential medium reading is to provide evidence, so the person knows you are bringing through their loved one. When you *know* their loved one, it can be challenging to have enough information to provide that isn't something you already know. Also, some mediums find it more difficult to read for people they know because they doubt whether the information coming through is from their own subconscious mind or if it is from spirit. Trusting in your abilities and trusting in spirit are key to delivering your readings. Trust is probably the most profound word having to do with your development and the delivery of your messages.

It is important not to jump into interpreting the evidence and message too quickly. If you interpret incorrectly, the sitter may dismiss you and start saying "no," which may throw you off entirely. Know that you may hear a "no," especially in the beginning. Do not let that deter you from everything you're receiving. For example, if you say you see a certain car, and the sitter isn't sure if that means anything, *describe* what you see. If they still don't understand, could this just be a person who was really into cars? Be open to what you get. Figuring it out will only help you in future readings.

I suggest first describing what you receive, whether it is a feeling, picture, or word. Just say exactly what you are getting. Usually, that will be understood. If not, then go into things you *feel* it could stand for or mean. It will almost always be one of those two things. I mentioned having had a symbol that took me an entire year to understand, because I only ever said what I was seeing, and never took the time to think about what the symbol *stood* for. I had to laugh when I figured it out.

Spirit uses the quickest way to get us a message, and it completely depends on how you best receive information and which clairs work best for you. Spirit is extremely clever and will help you in any way they can. If you see your neighbor Joe, does that mean the spirit's name is Joe, or does it mean the spirit who is coming through is the sitter's neighbor?

I suggest using the words "Spirit is showing me…" or "I am feeling…" or "Spirit is telling me…" You have to use your intuition, but you need to figure it out based on feedback from your sitter.

If you are unsure of something, you can always ask spirit to give it to you in another way, using another clair. Sometimes, it can take several readings to figure out what spirit is giving you. This is all part of the development process. You don't start out writing with your first word being *Mississippi.* It was more than likely a small two- or three-letter word, and you grew from there. Spirit knows that you are learning and growing and will always show up if you are committed to developing your abilities.

The whole point of giving a message is to help the sitter understand that their loved one is truly with them. Giving them evidential information is important for two reasons. The first is so the person knows that you are in fact connecting with their loved one. The second is so you can provide a message. It would be hard for the sitter to just receive a message if they didn't trust that you had their person in spirit with you, because anyone could just make up a message to pass on. Having evidence makes the message much more impactful.

In general, the less information you know about your sitter, or their loved ones in spirit, the better. This helps them by providing validation. When the sitter knows you have no previous information about their loved ones, it can provide much more healing and relief from grief, because they know there is no other way for you to have gotten the information. Try to present several pieces of information before asking for validation, so the sitter knows you are not just guessing, but actually delivering a message.

To avoid having the sitter give you too much information, ask them to tell you if they understand by saying, "yes," "no," or "maybe." When they get excited and know you are connected with their loved one, some of them will want to tell stories, but this can take you out of your reading brain and preemptively feed you information that spirit may have brought up that could have made the reading more impactful. You can have them interact and talk about what you have already brought up, but ask them not to tell you anything you haven't yet said. This too will help provide evidence.

Common evidential pieces of information are identity: mom, dad, brother, sister, cousin, friend, aunt, or uncle; the way they passed away, or health conditions they dealt with; physical traits; personality traits; age; name; habits; jobs; hobbies; loved ones here on Earth; current happenings; words and phrases they used; how they dressed; special memories; signs you attribute to them; and items that were important to them that have been passed down or left behind. The message is the most important part of the reading, but as I stated earlier, unless you provide evidential information, they may not trust the message you deliver.

Common messages are on topics of sorrow or regret for things they didn't say or do, support for decisions the loved ones had to make around the person in spirit's care, or thanks for the care you provided. They may want to make amends, apologize for things they did or said, say "thank you", "you made the right decision", "I love you" or "I'm proud of you." They may want to validate a dream or experience the sitter had. Or maybe the spirit wants to support the sitter in their struggles, like a death or job loss. Or it could be to celebrate an occasion, like a new baby, a wedding, or graduation. The goal of this message is to help the sitter live in more joy, release some burden of grief, and live a freer and happier life. Most of all, readings are for the sitter to know that the loved one in spirit is still with them.

I have been told one of the purposes of life and living is to enjoy every moment and to learn to be free of a lot of the things we have picked up or held onto, or which have weighed us down. Spirit wants us to live and experience as much life, love and joy as we can while we're here, and also to experience all the great things *they* may have missed out on. Spirit knows that we all have learning, healing, and growing to do (another main reason we come here). But to live freely is one of the best things you can do for your soul. You get to experience life in a different way in doing so.

CHAPTER FOURTEEN

Steps for a Successful Reading

"Believe in yourself, your abilities and your own potential.
Never let self-doubt hold you captive. You are worthy of all
that you dream of and hope for."
~ Roy Bennet

Something important to remember is that some readings hold a lot of information, and not all of it is happy. Trust that everything that comes through is meant for the highest good and the most healing possible. We are only here to help deliver the message, no matter what comes through. Know that what you are doing is making an impact.

Also, be sure you don't withhold any information. It can be scary if you get touchy or health-related information for the sitter. Know that if it comes up in the reading, it is meant to be delivered. Be sure to tell the sitter it is not meant to scare them, but to get ahead of a possible health problem. Assure them that spirit is here to help in any way they can. Suggest that they see a doctor and let them know spirit only helps with things we can control, in order to help the sitter have a better outcome.

Be sure you carry compassion when delivering messages. Sitters will often hold onto this information for a long time.

I strongly suggest that you keep your readings confidential and private. Judgment should be left at the door. We are here to help heal people, and judging anyone's situation or what they are going through will cloud your mind, making it harder to give clear messages.

I also suggest keeping a sitter's mediumship readings to no more frequently than every three months, but use your judgment regarding frequency. Some people may be going through a spiritual crisis or truly need help. Usually, the sitter needs to have time to live and heal between readings. When they are constantly coming in for readings, it can make it hard for them to really live. They may become too concerned with what is going on with their loved ones in spirit or want answers so they can do everything "right." If you feel people are getting too attached to the outcome of the readings, it's a good indicator that you should suggest they take some time away from readings and try making their own decisions. There is no real *right* path in life. You might want to mention that they are here to live and learn, and that is the beauty of life.

In some cases, you will know if the person is meant to get a reading or needs true help, and sometimes you will need to refer someone to a therapist or counselor. You'll intuitively know the difference.

The following steps will help you set up a framework for a successful reading:

1. Identify yourself and talk to the sitter to help them feel at ease. I usually ask them if they have had a reading before. Then tell your sitter what you do and how you receive information.
2. Ask them to avoid talking about anything you haven't yet brought up.
3. Say a prayer and let spirit know you are ready to connect.
4. Connect with spirit.
5. Identify who you are connecting with.
6. Interview spirit, asking questions such as:
   - Who are they?
   - Did they deal with any illnesses?
   - What were they like in life?
   - What were their passions?
   - How did they look?
   - How old were they?
   - Did they have family?

- What was their name?
- What were their greatest joys in life?
- Are they with any family on the other side?
- Do they have family here on Earth they want to mention?
- Are there any significant life events they want to mention being present for after their passing?
- What messages do they have to pass on?

7. Give the gathered information to the sitter.
8. Deliver the messages from spirit. What does spirit want to say to their loved one?
9. Close the reading and thank spirit and the sitter.

CHAPTER FIFTEEN

After the Reading

"Self-care is giving the world the best of you instead of what's left of you."
~ Katie Reed

Self-care is imperative when you are using your energy to help tune in to others and spirit's energy. It is just as important to be sure to disconnect after reading to ensure that you are not carrying any energy from the reading into your own life.

One way to know if this is happening is if you continue to think about the information that was coming through after the reading. Intentionally being aware of that should be enough to help in disconnecting from it. Taking a bath or going outside to get some fresh air can help refresh your energy. While some mediums feel that reading takes their energy, others feel that reading helps them feel energized, since they are connected to a higher-vibrational energy source.

I now find that individual and group readings are usually energizing for me, even if I have several in a row. As I mentioned earlier, that wasn't always the case. It's more about balancing your energy. I do sometimes find myself needing to relax afterward, to take a few minutes for myself to disconnect. It really just depends on the energy of the group and what types of readings they were.

Keep in mind that every person who shows up to a group reading more than likely has several spirit people in attendance. That is a lot of people to connect to, especially when emotions are involved.

Psychic readings may take more energy than mediumship readings. This is because you are tuning in to other people's energy and tend to help people address issues they may be dealing with. When you are tuning in to the issues, struggles, and challenges people are working to overcome, you pick up on some of the emotions involved. Let's be real: life can be hard sometimes.

If you are empathic or clairsentient, you will probably find the above to be especially true. Many of you have probably experienced this prior to your development. You may pick up on others' emotions, such as anxiety, or have had a hard time separating others' feelings from your own. Just sitting and relaxing for a bit or having a snack helps you reenergize.

Many mediums feel that a snack or something to eat after reading is needed. Some even like to have a glass of wine or a drink afterward, as it helps to disconnect from all of the energy they were connecting to. I find that stepping outside and getting some fresh air, with my feet on the ground (barefoot if you can, but just being outdoors helps), really helps me to reconnect and cleanse my energy from the previous client.

If you are doing back-to-back readings, I recommend that you have at least fifteen to twenty minutes between readings to disconnect from the previous one and then connect to the next sitter. When you are in reading mode, you are in the mental space and energy of spirit. I sometimes get a spacy or floaty feeling when I am overly tuned in, because it requires being in a different headspace. Having a snack or a glass of water or doing something completely unrelated to spirit or mediumship helps.

Why does that happen? I mentioned earlier about how our brain waves work. Studies of mediums and psychics who have been connected to electrodes show that they are able to consciously switch their brains over to a theta wave, which others only really experience during meditation or when falling asleep. Theta waves slow the brain down, so it can start receiving information in a reading. But it can be a tad difficult to move back and forth between communicating with humans and being tuned in to spirit too many times throughout the day. For that reason, I like to lump my readings together with small breaks between them and not have them too spaced out.

Just know that self-care is always needed when you are in the profession of helping others. Helping others is so much easier and rewarding when you are feeling good yourself.

I also want to talk about "over-reading." When you start reading for others and find out how healing it is for them, many people find themselves wanting to do more. You will find a good balance for you based on how you are feeling, and you'll know when you have overdone it. Take it easy. Start slowly and build your way up, paying attention to how each reading affects you and how you feel afterward.

CHAPTER SIXTEEN

A Reading Example

*"Spread love everywhere you go. Let no one ever come to
you without leaving happier."*
~ Mother Teresa

I am going to give you an example of how a reading may be put together, so you are aware of some of the evidential pieces of information that should be brought through prior to delivering the message. The more evidential the reading is, the better. All readings are different, and some may be more heartfelt, while some really deliver on the evidence of the afterlife or connection to the sitter. No matter which way the reading unfolds, trust that what comes through is exactly what needs to come through.

This example of a reading is provided to demonstrate the structure and flow of providing some evidence and giving a message. All readings are different, but seeing how they piece together is important, because all readings should have a flow.

Sample Reading

Medium: Hi, there! How are you today? My name is Sarah, and I am a psychic medium. I'm here to help you to connect with your loved ones in spirit, by giving spirit a voice, to help bring you comfort in knowing that your loved ones in spirit are around you. Our goal is to bring you evidential information, giving you peace of mind in knowing that your loved ones are still around and watching over you from heaven.

Sitter: Hi, I'm Julie. Nice to meet you. I'm doing well today, very excited!

Medium: Have you ever had a reading before, or how did you find me? [Ask questions to help lighten the mood. This is important, because most sitters come to their readings nervous. The less nervous they are, the better the energy is for the reading. With small talk, they soon realize you are quite normal, there is nothing to worry about, and they start to relax.]

Medium: I receive information through all of my extra senses—hearing, seeing, and feeling—and I will, to the best of my ability, translate everything for you. If you understand what I'm saying during the reading, you can confirm with a yes or no and share what you understand. Try not to tell me anything I have not yet stated. That takes me out of my reading mind and puts me into my thinking mind and can interfere with the reading and you getting validation. Do you have any questions?

Sitter: Nope, I'm ready.

Medium: I have a young male stepping forward, who is identifying himself as a son. [Remember, by using your clairs, you can ask for validation if the spirit hasn't given this to you yet. I always ask spirit to identify themselves in relation to the sitter, because I find it easiest: mom, dad, grandma, grandpa, brother, sister, friend, aunt, uncle, etc. Some use a more generic terms, which is okay too, such as "young male" or "motherly female." Just be aware that these days, some spirits are nonbinary, and that may come through as well. This has happened to me in readings, and I was a bit confused, but said what I was getting, which helped the sitter have even more validation.]

Sitter: Yes, I understand. I lost my son.

Medium: He is telling me that he passed suddenly, and his passing was unexpected.

Sitter: Yes.

Medium: He is telling me that he passed in a car accident and is taking accountability for his actions around his passing. He is telling me that he liked to party a bit too much. Can you understand this?

Sitter (tearful): Yes, he went out after a party and was drinking and driving, so that makes sense.

Medium: I am so very sorry for your loss. He is showing me that he visits another male, who ended up injured, but survived the accident. He is showing me the male he is with struggles with this.

Sitter: That is correct. The other boy, his best friend, survived, and I know he had a hard time for quite a while.

Medium: He wants you to know that he is taking accountability for what happened that night. He just wasn't thinking but wants everyone to know that he is at peace, and no one else should blame themselves for what happened.

Sitter: Thank you, I needed to hear this. I know there's nothing we could have done, but it's hard not to wish we would have done something different and not let him go out that night.

Medium: I do want to share that he is quite chatty, so I know that he loved talking. He seems flirty and mentions he loved being the center of attention. [This statement lightens the mood and makes the sitter smile. Spirit is quite smart and knows that the entirety of the reading should not be full of heavy information. They bring in things to make people laugh and smile, to help them remember the positive aspects too.]

Sitter: Yes, that is definitely my son! He loved being the center of attention!

Medium: Would you understand that he liked playing practical jokes on people and enjoyed laughing? He really enjoyed making everyone laugh.

Sitter: Yes, he was funny and always loved a good practical joke.

Medium: He is mentioning that he has a sister and that he is around her often. He tells me she's going through some changes right now with her work situation.

Sitter: Yes, he has a sister, and she is changing jobs. She has been taking classes for a while now and has finally graduated and gotten a job offer at her dream corporation. She is so happy!

Medium: If his sister is open to it, her brother would love to let her know that he is aware of her career changes and is around her often.

Sitter: She would love to know this and misses her brother so much. I will pass this on.

Medium: He mentions being with a small lap dog. Two colors, light. I see white and beige.

Sitter: Yes! We just lost our family dog, Candy, who was Maltese, white-and-beige coloring. She was such a sweet dog, and we miss her so. That makes me so happy to know they are together!

Medium: She is full of energy, and I see her jumping up and down.

Sitter: Yes, that is definitely her! Running circles around us until the day she left us.

Medium: He is telling me he is with your mom and dad.

Sitter: Yes, they are both on the other side as well.

Medium: He is mentioning you feeling like you didn't tell him you loved him enough. He is telling me to tell you to stop that. He always felt loved by you so much and doesn't want you beating yourself up. You were a good mom.

Sitter (crying): Yes, I question that every day. I'm so glad he brought this up, because I asked him to mention this if he felt that I was a good mom.

Medium: How neat is that for your son to come through, trying to help you understand that you were everything you needed to be and could be for him? That is the true essence of love: helping others see that they are perfect in their own way, despite self-judgment or worrying about being good enough.

Sitter: Amazing.

Medium: He is showing me a small box that has a letter and a piece of jewelry—a thick silver chain.

Sitter: Yes, I found a letter he wrote to me as a young boy, and I have the necklace that he wore every day. A big silver chain.

Medium: Validation that your son is aware of the items of his that you have kept.

Sitter: That's amazing, because I asked him to mention this!

Medium: He tells me that, since he has passed, there's a space between you and your husband, and he isn't a fan of what's going on. He wants you two to be happy.

Sitter: Yes, after our son passed, my husband and I haven't been talking much. I want to, but we're so caught up in our grief. I'm not sure why we've let ourselves do this, but I'll let my husband know. I'll try and talk to him more about how I'm feeling. I think he would feel better talking about our son as well.

Medium: Your son is telling me that he knows you don't feel like you should be happy after his passing, that you almost feel bad about the days you start to feel better, and he wants you to be happy.

Sitter: Yes. I think that's why me and my husband have stopped talking as much. I am so grateful for these messages, and I plan to take the steps to try to reconnect to my husband. We need it.

Medium: That is so great! Know that your son will be with you every step of the way. You will always miss your son. Grief is a lifelong process. Know that your son wants you to be happy, and he knows you miss him, but you will see him again one day. He is always with you, and you are able to talk to him whenever you want. He can hear you, your thoughts, and he sees everything you're doing, even though you cannot see him. Ask for a message from him and know that it will happen. One last thing as we're wrapping up: he wants to send a quick hi to someone named Cory, if you could pass that on as well?

Sitter: Yes, that's his best friend you mentioned earlier. I will absolutely pass that on, thank you so much!

Close the reading. Thank spirit for showing up and say goodbye to the sitter.

Note: This example is quite condensed, but I wanted to give a quick run-through of a short reading. If this were a real reading, I would go into a connection with her parents as well. Every now and then, you will have a spirit hop in just to say hi, if you have already connected to several. But in this instance, I knew her mom and dad would absolutely have information to come through that the sitter would love to hear.

CHAPTER SEVENTEEN

Gaining Confidence in Your Readings

*"A flower does not think of competing with the flower next to it,
it just blooms."*
~ Zen Shin

Once you understand the layout of readings, you are ready to start giving practice readings. Putting the outline of a reading together is important, but you need to practice and deliver many readings until you fully understand your spirit dictionary. Once you learn how to do this, I strongly recommend joining a development circle, or doing practice readings with people you know or with other developing mediums.

There is no replacement for having someone in front of you to read and get real-time validation from. This allows you to verify your spirit signs and words. Consistently reading is a great way to help you step into your confidence as your medium/psychic self. You will see that it is a process and can take some time. Over time, as you grow your spirit dictionary, you will find that the same words, images, and feelings start to show up. This is why doing practice readings is so important. You will also begin to trust spirit more, because you realize that they always show up when you are ready to give a reading. You will also develop more trust in the information that is coming through.

I remember, in my early development, getting information that would come up that seemed odd or unusual to me, so I would hold onto it for fear of being wrong. After the reading, I would talk to the sitter, and they would mention the exact thing about the person I'd been fearful of saying! After this happened several times, I learned how imperative it is to say absolutely everything you receive, even if you don't understand the meaning or it seems odd. More than likely, it will be a neat piece of evidential information, and honestly, those are the ones that make for the best evidential readings.

Trust and confidence are two of the harder things' mediums must work on. It's important for you to know that you can trust, and that spirit has a higher knowing for the things they choose to bring to the reading. They also want their loved ones here on Earth to have peace of mind, to know that our souls live on, and that they are still around us. Please know that this is a process and something that happens with consistent practice.

When you want to develop a certain area of your readings, you can always ask spirit to help you work on that. When you see that information starts to come through, you will know spirit is truly helping you, which helps to build your trust. When you have that knowledge and can maintain giving a full thirty-minute-to-one-hour reading, you are probably ready to advance to doing readings professionally if you choose.

Some people think that mediums step out confidently with their gifts without any training or practice, like they see in the people on television. I have had a few famous television mediums as teachers, and I can tell you firsthand that they too have had to deal with working on and developing their self-confidence.

I do want to talk for a second about naysayers. Some people will tell you that communicating with souls on the other side is evil or fake. More than likely it's what they have been taught or they haven't had a spiritual encounter. Some people can't open their minds to it. Don't let it sway what you know to be true. I'm not sure what evil could possibly have to do with something that brings so much love, healing, and light into the world, but I can tell you that you don't do this work to convince anyone of anything they are not ready to understand. It is a complete waste of your time. You know what is true, and that is all that matters. I feel that admitting that you communicate with "dead people" (or souls, as I prefer to say) is hard enough. Let people know of your abilities at the right time *for you*. It is honestly a process of owning your confidence. I can promise you that speaking up and owning all of you, and allowing your light to shine, is a huge growing process. You will be so much more thankful and free when you are able to do so and do it with confidence. If people don't support you, then they honestly aren't your people. The right ones will show up for you and absolutely adore the real you.

Making sure that you stay true to yourself, regardless of others' opinions or feedback, is extremely important. Confidence takes time. With continued connection and positive validation, you will see that your readings grow, and your confidence is truly not about how others see what you do or even confirmation that the information that you are giving is correct. It is more about knowing that what you are getting is true, and your connection to your abilities and spirit is far more than any confirmation anyone could give you. We are naturally divine beings, and connection to all things physical and nonphysical is truly who we are to the core. Perceiving and receiving information from spirit is in our true essence.

CHAPTER EIGHTEEN

Medical Information

"What happens when people open their hearts? They get better."
~ Haruki Murakami

When medical information comes up during readings, mediums may feel skeptical about passing this information on. How the spirit person passed usually comes through as an identifier, or for a significant reason. I'm talking more about information that comes up that needs to be passed on to the person you are giving the reading to.

For me, this happens quite often. I think it may be because of my nursing background. I feel spirit has a broad spectrum of health information to pull from with me, so I'm able to use that in readings. I remember being leery of passing on information about health screenings, labs, and other medical issues. But if it comes up in the reading, it is meant to be passed on.

In pretty much every reading, spirit will come through with an identifier of how they passed. They may bring up health-related information as a push for the sitter to be screened for the same illness the spirit may have dealt with in life. This mostly happens in readings where the person in spirit has brought up that they were not on top of taking care of their health and didn't do proper preventative screenings.

They may take accountability for their passing because they knew they were dealing with a health issue and simply chose not to go to a doctor for treatment. They want better for their loved one.

There is almost always a correlation. Over time, you will start to learn what information is about spirit and what is for the living person. It will feel different, and your attention will be directed at the person getting the reading if it is not about the spirit person.

I will feel things in my body that tell me things about another person's body. I may hear spirit say things, like "son," "congenital," and "heart check." This lets me know that, even if the son is not present for the reading, I need to bring this up to the sitter who is here connecting to their father.

Often, health information that comes up is for someone who is not present in the reading, but is information the sitter can validate, because they know things about the person in question, and they can pass a message on. One example of what I might tell them is "I need to say, I have Dad here, who is saying there may be a familial link with a heart condition. So, it is important for your brother, or your dad's son, to go to preventative screenings."

Most times, I mirror the person, and I will feel their illness in my body. For instance, I can tell if someone has left knee pain or an injury because my left knee will start to hurt. Or my back will start to hurt in the same spot they have back problems. It's the same for issues with the lungs, heart, or head. Other times, I see a map or outline of a person's body and can see a dark spot in a certain area, and I know I need to talk about that. Whatever way you receive this information, know that this specific spirit is working the best way they can to get the information to you to help their loved one.

I will never forget my first experience of passing on health-related information. I was connecting a lady to her granddaughter in spirit. Such beautiful, evidential information was coming through, and at the end of the reading, the granddaughter was giving me a message that there was something going on with her grandmother's head. I could see it, and I could feel it. The message I got was that it was not cancerous but needed to be checked by a physician. I very casually asked the lady if she had any knowledge of something that might be going on. We talked for a minute, and she told me she had excess fluid in her brain, and she was aware, and that she did try to make most of her checkups. I made sure to tell her I had a healthcare background and that I knew how important checkups are, and I stressed the importance of them before giving her love from her granddaughter and closing the reading.

Around four o'clock the next morning, I was awoken by this young girl's voice. I immediately knew it was the young girl who I had connected to the evening prior. She was showing me the "caution" sign and reminded me of the conversation I'd had with her grandma, the night before. I knew she wanted her grandma to go to the doctor sooner than the next checkup, which was several months away. I was hesitant, as I had never passed anything medical on before, but I messaged the lady and told her what I was seeing, and that I felt she needed to go to the doctor sooner rather than later for a checkup. She agreed, so I felt more at peace and knew I had said what I needed to say.

Two weeks later, I got a message from the lady saying that two days after I reached out to her, she had a massive seizure and had to go to the hospital to have stents placed to drain fluid buildup within her brain. She had to be placed in a medically induced coma for a week to let her brain rest.

As nervous as I was to pass this information on, there was a purpose greater than me. After that experience, I vowed to always trust spirit with that type of information. I pass it on to sitters, letting them know it is not to instill fear, but to try to help them improve their health and prevent further issues. I have personally had numerous readings where things like this have been brought up. I have also found that most mediums have this type of information come up from time to time, even if they don't have special knowledge around biology. Trust in spirit, knowing that they have much larger sight and knowledge than we do. They are most definitely here supporting and helping us in so many ways, including helping us to take better care of ourselves.

Remember to deliver this kind of information with empathy. Make sure to let the sitter know this information only comes up to help, or to prevent something in some way. It is most important to state that you are not a physician, and you are not here to diagnose anything, ever. You are here to simply pass on the information you are getting, so the sitter can do with the information what they choose. Whether that may be to follow up with a long-overdue health screening or see a doctor for a possible health issue that they may be dealing with.

CHAPTER NINETEEN

Grief

"The reality is that you will grieve forever. You will not "get over" the loss of a loved one; you'll learn to live with it. You will heal and you will rebuild yourself around the loss you have suffered. You will be whole again, but you will never be the same. Nor should you be the same, nor would you want to."
~ Elizabeth Kubler-Ross

Grief is an extremely complicated emotion, a natural emotional and physical response to any type of grief or loss. It can feel overwhelming and all-encompassing at the same time. It is important to learn about grief when developing your mediumship, because you will be dealing with people in various stages of it, to help address these emotions and approach them with understanding and empathy.

It is common that many people come into their mediumship because of having dealt with some trauma or loss of their own loved one. This can help tremendously with understanding that grief is not the same as being sad for a few months. Grief can be described as an onion. It's an unraveling that may stay or come and go and will most definitely be ongoing as one deals with the many different layers.

Everyone's experience with grief is different, and no two people heal in the same way. The level of grief you experience will be different, depending on the closeness and relationship you had with the loved one who has passed on. Obviously, the closer the relationship, the harder someone usually grieves, keeping in mind that some people naturally don't tune in to their emotions as much as others and may not experience the same levels of grief as someone who does. Or they may not appear to anyway, and this doesn't mean they aren't processing it internally. We either process or store grief, and I have found there to be a physical correlation for people who do not openly express their emotions to someone.

I say this carefully, because I personally believe that these people don't necessarily grieve *less*, but may compartmentalize their grief, in order to be able to get through the days, weeks, and life in general. It may not necessarily always come out in the form of grief, but perhaps in other ways. I hold no judgment, because I have been through my own grief, and I handled it in many different ways at different times, which can be expected during any grieving process. The most important thing to take away is that all forms of grief are completely normal.

For many people, grief can be quite a feat to learn to live with. This is especially true for someone who has lost a really close family member, who has lost someone tragically, or has unresolved questions. *How can I go on without them? I don't want to go on without them. Why did my loved one have to pass in such a traumatic way? Did they suffer? Why did they take their own life? If only we could have a redo of our last minutes together, I would have done everything so differently. Why did I not know more about what they were going through? Why did they not talk to me? Why did my loved one have to struggle with a certain illness? Why did my loved one have to go? Why did I say those things to them? If only we had resolved that issue. If only we could have said goodbye. If only I'd told them I loved them. If only I could have seen them one last time, I would have done that differently. I wish we'd had a closer relationship. I wish they had talked to me about what they were dealing with. I wish it was me and not them.*

These are just some of the things that make grieving hard. It is common for people to experience these questions at different times. Other's may experience "survivor's guilt." They feel they should not be experiencing joy without their loved one. This is something that may come up in a reading, especially if they lost someone traumatically. It's important to let them know that any way the person grieves is normal and okay. One day they may be feeling okay and the next it's hard to get out of bed and function. There is no timeline. Grief is versatile, and no one way is right or wrong. It is different for everyone. Having compassion for themselves and how they are feeling is imperative in moving through grief.

It is always a medium's goal to help make their sitter's days better by connecting them to their loved ones. Mediumship is a great way for people to get a little piece of healing and validation. Hopefully, their connections are able to help them get through their days a bit more easily, and maybe even bring a bit of a spark back to their life.

Usually, messages apply to whatever the sitter may be going through or holding onto that is unresolved. We can help them understand that our souls live on, and that they will one day be reunited with their loved one. Let them know they too can talk to their loved ones and tune in if they choose.

CHAPTER TWENTY

Connection to Your Own Loved Ones in Spirit

"I will hold you in my heart until I can hold you again in heaven."
~ Author Unknown

Something I feel is really important to know and remember is that we all innately carry the ability to communicate and connect with our psychic and mediumship abilities. We are spirit living in a physical body. For people who don't believe they can tune in to their loved ones, it can seem like a far reach. I'm here to tell you it's not.

My grandma passed when I was only seven years old, and I have found I have had an even closer connection to her since developing my mediumship. She shows up in all of the readings I personally have had done, and every now and then, I'm reminded of the memories of her through random sights, smells, and words and phrases that I hear in my day to day and in my dreams. She is very much around me.

This really is about knowing and trusting that you feel drawn to connecting to spirit or your psychic abilities for a reason, just as some are drawn to the business world, culinary field, or any other job or activity they desire to connect to. If you are drawn to healing and the metaphysical, trust that you innately have these abilities. Not everyone chooses to do this work professionally, but trust that no matter the reason you are drawn to this, it will help you in one way or another—either by tuning in to your abilities to make *your* own life decisions easier, to tune in to and connect to your own loved ones, or to do this professionally. Regardless, you are here to grow your abilities and will know what path is right for you.

Spirits absolutely line up, first and foremost, to connect directly to their loved ones in spirit. They try, in most ways, to show up and reach their living loved ones through dreams, signs, music, feelings, or images that may be recalled. Many write these experiences off as just remembering their loved one or a daydream, hoping their loved one is around them. However, because most people tend to write these experiences off as coincidence, spirits are always ready and willing to connect to people through mediums.

Time on the other side is different. It's not measured the same way, but spirit is knowledgeable and can see ahead in time and know that their loved ones will be booking a reading with a medium. Spirit will often even come through ahead of time with information for the reading coming up. Once you begin reading, you will see how this happens. Mediumship is not a special talent, but truly something you can choose to grow and develop, like a muscle.

The simplest way for most mediums and psychics to tune in to their abilities, especially in the beginning, is through meditation, which we talked about back in Chapter Three. Meditation is the easiest way in the beginning to get in touch with the clearing and slowing down of the daily clutter we put our minds through. Over time, you will see that it becomes much more of a "changing the channel" and tuning into the meditative state that makes it easy for spirit to step in without you even meditating. Meditation opens the connection and will teach you how to be aware of spirits and how you tune in when they are stepping in. When you tune in, it begins to sensitize you to spirit, and everything you sense will begin to make sense.

This is why doing practice readings is so important. It allows you to train your brain to reach that higher level of consciousness much faster. Early on in development, many mediums may feel they need to meditate prior to connection. Over time, it might be a practice you want to keep, just because of its benefits. But it is not truly needed to connect, because your brain is trained, and you tune in without even trying.

Before I fully tuned into my mediumship, I was just having connections here and there. I really wanted to see if I could connect to my grandma, if I could intentionally reach out to someone and have them step in, not just let spirit step in when *they* wanted to reach out. But by doing this, I unknowingly opened up to lots spirits—loved ones, friends, patients, the list goes on. I meditated a few times a week for about ten minutes at a time, and that was plenty for me. Now I only meditate for about ten minutes a couple of times a *month*, and I only really do that if I am feeling like I need to relax or disconnect from the daily stress of my life. That, or when I'm feeling disconnected from my spiritual practices. More often than not, I don't even meditate at all, and yet I find that my readings have grown stronger. I have learned how to raise my vibration, so to speak, to connect to spirit.

For the average person, it is important to pay attention to signs and dreams. If spirit really wants to connect during the waking hours, it is more than likely going to begin during meditation or a time when you are relaxing in the evening or at night, when they know you are going to be more receptive. Either that, or when you are going through tough times and really needing their support. I am going to walk us through a meditation for tuning into your own loved ones, which you may pass on to your clients.

Meditation to connect to your own loved ones in spirit.
Gently close your eyes. Get into a comfortable position, either sitting or lying down. Take a deep breath in and count to four. Hold to the count of four. Exhale to the count of four. Focus on relaxing.

If you notice any thoughts coming in, either imagine them floating up on a balloon to heaven or floating away on a leaf down a river. Continue to breathe to counts of four and focus on relaxing. Say the word "relax" if you need help doing this. Feel how comfortable you are. If there is any part of you that is uncomfortable, imagine your breath coming into your lungs and going to that specific area, relieving it of any discomfort.

Keep breathing to counts of four. Imagine a bright light shining down on you from heaven. Imagine the light shining so brightly that you become part of it. You see a beautiful garden in front of you. The sun is shining, and it is a warm day. There are bushes sculpted into designs, and flowers gently blowing in the wind. So many different colors to see. You see yellow and white butterflies flying around. Bees are buzzing around, pollinating the flowers. Tall maple trees and willow trees blow in the soft breeze. You catch the smell of all of the flowers, a sweet whiff of rose and lilac bushes. The sun shines down on you, making you feel comfortable and warm, relaxed. You hear different little birds chirping all around you.

You continue walking into this big garden and come upon a fountain, so pretty and peaceful. You listen to the water flowing. You are in an amazing state of peace, consumed with the serenity of everything you are taking in. You take a deep breath, breathing in peace and letting out all forms of stress. You are relaxed.

You see pillow-like stairs made of fluffy clouds. You know that if you approach the stairs, you will be connecting to one of your loved ones on the other side. You approach the stairs, knowing that you will soon be seeing a loved one that you dearly miss and are excited to connect with.

You begin slowly yet excitedly walking to the stairs and taking the first step up. You take another and another, slowly walking up the twisting, billowy staircase. With each step, your excitement is building. You take a total of twelve steps and see a bench waiting atop a pillowy cloud. Butterflies are fluttering around. You still feel the breeze, smell the scent of flowers, and hear the birds chirping in the background. You take a seat on the bench, knowing that your loved one will soon be joining you.

You sit and wait, enjoying the pleasant sunshine, scenery, and smells. You suddenly feel the presence of someone walking up behind you. They take a seat next to you on the bench. They reach out and grab your hand. You feel an overwhelming sense of love just from their touch.

They have so much to catch you up on. They have been wanting you to know they have been around you. They have seen all the things you have been through and want you to know that they too have been there with you, alongside you on your journey, by your side in spirit. They have shared your laughter and joy. They have seen your pain and sorrow. They have been with you through everything. They have an important message to tell you. What do they want to say to you to help you on your life journey? Take your time. What do you discuss?

You sit with them for a while longer, just experiencing the joy of being together, sharing everything, however it may be communicated. Take all the time you need here.

Your loved one must return to the spirit world now. You have had an amazing time connecting. Your loved one gives you a hug and turns to leave. They leave you with a farewell and a knowing that they will be around you again soon. There is one specific message they wish to leave you with. What is it?

You watch them disappear into a beam of light from heaven, shining so brightly and full of love. You turn around and start walking down the stairs slowly, reminiscing about your meet-up. With pure love, you return to the garden. You again become mesmerized by the beauty of your surroundings, the peacefulness of the sights, sounds, and smells. You take a deep breath in again, counting to four, holding for four, exhaling for four. You continue to breathe deeply, taking in the beautiful messages you just received, and the time spent with your loved one. You are at peace, knowing they are at peace. You continue breathing for counts of four.

You begin to connect more to your physical surroundings. You feel the bed, couch, or floor beneath you. You hear the sounds of the room you are in. You keep breathing and now remember that you are no longer in the garden, but here in the physical world. You connect more to your surroundings and begin moving your fingers and toes. Count to four and open your eyes.

Some people, at this point, feel they should write down the messages that were communicated by their loved one. What did your loved one have to say? It should have some meaning and hopefully bring some peace or healing to you.

You can repeat this exercise as many times as you need. It may take a time or two to connect. Part of this is your own mental blockage that you have created by doubting that your loved one actually might come through to you and that you are in fact having encounters.

If this exercise only took you five minutes, and you feel you didn't make a connection or receive a message, try again. You may want to spend more time on the four-four-four breathing, to make sure you are more relaxed. Or spend more time taking in the garden and scenery, until you are able to detach from your daily thoughts. Wait until your mind is still and at peace before you begin climbing the stairs. These tips should help you to become more relaxed and receptive.

It is important to trust in your connection. Some people will feel like they are making it up. You aren't. I too remember that feeling. It is important for you to know that heaven doesn't exist in some faraway place.

You can use this meditation when you want to connect, but you can also ask for signs from your loved one that you can receive throughout your day. The more you trust, the more you will receive and grow. Remember that once you transition, your soul is in the world of consciousness and energy. It is different from anything we experience here on Earth. Allow and receive.

Once you have made the connection, over time, you will see it is much easier to connect than you first thought, and you'll see that your loved ones begin to step in on their own from time to time. Or perhaps they always have, and you are just relearning that it is possible to have a connection with them, even though they are in heaven and you on Earth. I think it is more of a relearning—or unlearning—of things we have been taught throughout life.

CHAPTER TWENTY-ONE

Dreams

*"And if I cannot find you while I am awake, I will visit you in my dreams
so often that it will become second nature to imagine you here with me."*
~ Noor Shirazie

Dreams are a common way for our loved ones in spirit to reach us.
The state your brain is in right before you fall asleep, or right before
waking up, makes it easier for your loved ones to step in and connect.
This is because your mind has disconnected from all the thoughts of the
day, and it hasn't yet had the chance to begin making to-do lists for the
new day. Most people say this is usually when they have dream visits
from their loved ones.

It's important to know that if you experience a dream of a loved one
that has anything to do with fear, suffering, or something scary, then it
is not a true dream visit from your loved one. That has more to do with
memories and fears that have been stored subconsciously. These feelings
and emotions regarding your loved one's death may need to be examined.
Many times, this has to do with fear that they suffered, or worrying that
they are not in heaven. This may have to do with unresolved emotions,
like sadness, regret, anger, or fear, either related to their passing or to
situations you may have dealt with in life related to your relationship
with them.

Any time you dream of your loved one and it creates feelings of peace, love, joy, or maybe just a bit of sadness, those emotions are due to knowing you had a connection with them during your dream state. Sometimes that experience creates more of a longing to see or reconnect with your loved one, but they usually leave you with a feeling of peace. Please know that this was an actual dream visitation.

In a dream visit, it is common for our loved ones to come through quite strongly. These are usually vivid dreams, and you will remember them. This happens for a reason. It is to let you know, and help you remember, that your loved one has in fact stepped in to visit you. Regular, everyday dreams are easily forgotten as soon as you wake and start to go about your day. When you have a dream visit, you remember it vividly, including the details in the dream, for weeks, months, and years to come. This impression stays with you much longer, to let you know that your loved one is around you and that you do have the ability to communicate and connect with them.

Pay attention to what is happening in your dream, as that is part of the message. Our loved ones tend to show up more when we are going through the ebbs and flows of life. This might be during a transition, wedding, graduation, death, birth, job change, divorce, move, or anything that causes stress, good or bad. They want to support us, just as they would have when they were here. If they would have picked up the phone to reach out while alive, or you would have wanted to reach out to them, know they are with you at those times.

There are common themes in dreams where our loved ones come through. Many times, people say their loved one didn't say anything, but stood there and watched them and what was happening within their dream. This is your loved one saying, loud and clear, that they are here and watching and supporting you. If they hugged you, know that they are aware of what you are going through in life, and they are wanting to send you a hug.

If you are talking with them, pay attention to everything they say to you, because there is a message in it. I have found there are also certain themes that happen with dream visits with loved ones. The most common is if there is water, know that it has to do with you processing emotions regarding something you're dealing with in waking life or that may have to do with their passing. If you are shopping in a mall or doing something with clothing, they are there supporting you through identity changes you are going through in life. Dreams about shopping or clothes also represent how we are seen by other people and how we outwardly express ourselves.

Sometimes, a simple touch or smile from them can say everything. Or they can give you advice, or warn you of danger, or to be aware of something that may be coming up in your life that you haven't been paying attention to.

Another way you will know that your loved one has stepped in is that they appear in their healthy and happy state. This is to send you the message that they are okay and pain free and not dealing with earthbound things they previously dealt with. If they appear with illness, or as they were when they passed, this has to do with your fears and anger or sadness around how they passed, and more than likely it was not a true visitation dream, but your subconscious mind still processing their passing.

You may have dreams with memories of things you experienced with your loved one. This is your loved one stepping in to remind you of positive memories they want you to remember. The message is "Please remember me and our happy times, not the things that you are holding onto regarding my passing."

Regular dreams usually leave us confused or trying to figure out the meaning or theme. But visitation dreams are clear and leave us feeling a sense of peace. Sometimes, a dream feels so real and vivid that you wake up absolutely knowing it was a visitation. However, sometimes you're jolted with the knowledge that your loved one has, in fact, just visited you, and it leaves you feeling sad. Trust me when I say that was not the purpose for their dream visit. They only wanted to comfort you and leave you feeling happier and more at peace.

Dream visits are a great way for the souls of your loved ones (humans and pets) to reach out to you and let you know that they are around and supporting you. I ask that you trust and always know that they will step in and give you support when you need it most. Our loved ones know when we need guidance, and maybe even more often when we are least expecting it. You will be impressed with their outreach for a long time to come. It's a special way for them to leave an imprint on our heart, even when they are no longer here in the physical world.

CHAPTER TWENTY-TWO

Signs from Spirit

*"Signs from spirit are all around us and everything speaks to us
if we are aware."*
~ James Van Praagh

"Signs from spirit" is a topic I love to talk to people about. Once you start to tune in and realize that you can ask your loved ones in spirit for a sign, you will see that we are much more guided and connected than we may have once thought. Spirit is extremely smart and connected to source and is aware of any ask that you may have of them. I like to say that spirit is literally just a thought away.

Spirits are pure consciousness and energy. They are no longer confined to a physical body, so they can show up and be present within a second. The reason behind asking for signs from spirit is that many people doubt what they pick up on from their loved one, whether it is something they see, hear, or feel. Sometimes, it is easier to ask for something tangible that we can see here in the physical world, which we can attribute to our loved one on the other side.

I love the metaphysical world, but I love science and how science is starting to tune into and show, through study after study, that energy is real. Science is not just physical. Studies have shown that thoughts create molecules that affect our energetic field.

I read about a study with cups of water, where participants were blindfolded and were asked to pick the water that tasted better. Both glasses had the exact same water in them. One cup had negative words and emotions written on it, and the other had positive affirmations written on it. The judges unanimously, blindly, picked the water that had positive affirmations written on it.

They did the same test in a petri dish, letting it sit for a week. After a week, the petri dish with negative words began turning into mold, whereas the one with positive words remained crystal clear. The Japanese researcher who conducted these experiments showed us that conscious intention affected the molecular structure of water. We are made of water!

I bring this up because I think it is important for people to understand. Science is proving that intention and action create and affect the energy around you. Anything you choose to focus on and put time and energy into will grow, and science has proven this. If you ask for your deceased loved one to show up, they absolutely will. If you choose to tune in to your mediumship and connection with the other side, it will grow.

Feelings or goose bumps are a common sign from spirit. You may feel as if you have been touched and find that you think of a specific loved one in spirit. I always say the first person who comes to mind when you experience your sign—it's them.

The same happens if you have a feeling first. You usually think of a specific person in spirit and know you are linking this together for a reason. You may be listening to a song or driving down the road and find that your mind is drifting off, thinking of a memory of your loved one, then you suddenly get full-body chills or an overwhelming sense of love. Know that this is absolutely your sensory system, which goes beyond the physical, picking up on your loved one in spirit.

As I am writing this, I'm thinking back to when my husband's mom passed away. It was a day or two after we heard of her unexpected passing, and it was just beginning to sink in. If you know what I am talking about, then you know it is a strange experience, understanding that you will not be hearing or seeing someone in the physical world again. Unfortunately, she lived in another state, so my husband and I were not able to be there at the time of her passing. (I am getting the chills as I write this, feeling her step in at this very second.) Yes, that is how fast your loved ones can step in when you think of them!

My husband and I were sitting on the couch in our living room, crying and talking about her passing, and my husband and I both got full-body chills. The energy in our small living room shifted. My husband very much supports me in my mediumship, but is more interested in sports, knowledge, trivia, and everything tangible in the world. At that moment, I asked him if he felt her around us, and he said yes. The hairs on our arms were standing up at the same time. We could feel her spirit so strongly, and we knew without a doubt she was there with us.

I've had experiences with spirit for as long as I can remember, but from that moment with my mother-in-law forward, my connection with spirit started to grow. I understood it differently. She was letting us know that she was still here and around us. It was more of a conscious connection than what I had put thought into before.

My husband isn't what I would consider "tuned in to spirit" at all. He wasn't trying to connect to spirit, but he had this experience with me simultaneously. How would one chalk that up to a coincidence when we were feeling and thinking the same thing? My husband and his mother talked absolutely every day, if not multiple times a day, so why would we expect that it would be different now, when she was in heaven? He needed her, and she knew it. Perhaps she is even freer, not bound to connect to anyone by a phone call, but able to be with us whenever she pleases. I have personally found that I have had this happen quite often during times when I am happy, sad, in need of support or wanting to talk to someone. Spirit has a divine intelligence. They know when you need them.

Music is another sign from our loved ones in spirit. Any time you hear a song that reminds you of your loved one in spirit, it is a sign from them that they are around. You might be driving down the road, feel the urge to change the station, and when you do, you suddenly hear your loved one's favorite song on the radio. Trust that you felt like changing the station for a reason. It is absolutely your loved one popping in to say hi, especially if you get an impression or think of them.

Maybe you listened to a song with your loved one around the time they passed, and that song now represents your loved one for you. When you hear it, and it connects you to them, know that it is a sign.

Flying things are also common signs from spirit. People attribute flying things to spirit because they are above the ground and closer to the heavens. Birds, butterflies, and dragonflies are just a few. Get specific with your sign, such as the color or type of butterfly. Make it something unique, so you trust it more. You will absolutely know what your sign is when you see it and connect to it. Then keep that as your specific sign for that specific spirit. It is easy to chalk up all red cardinals to being signs from spirit (and your sign may well be a cardinal), so don't deviate from that. But your sign can be literally anything. Pick a certain color and type of bird or butterfly, and know that when you see it, it is your loved one stepping in to say hi.

Numbers are another sign. You probably have had some sort of connection to numbers or a particular number coming up in your life as a sign. When you connect to a number, it should be something specific, like an athlete's jersey number, a birth date, or a number your loved one mentioned to you. Sometimes it's a number that you started seeing on a regular basis after your loved one passed away.

Imagine that you are driving down the road and stop at a red light. You are ready to take off and suddenly glance up at the license plate in front of you—not at the car or the person driving, but at the license plate. It just so happens to be the birth date of your husband who is in spirit. The number might be 112 if his birthday was January 12. Know that your loved one directed your attention to this, at that moment, for a reason. It was to give you a sign that he is still around and supporting you on your life's journey from the other side.

Names work in a similar way. If the same thing as above happened with the license plate, but it said your spouse's name, or showed his initials, and your attention was drawn to it, it was for the same reason. They are with you, trying to get your attention.

If you dismiss it, thinking it was a coincidence, and then end up in the grocery store checkout line behind someone wearing a jersey with your spouse's name on the back of it, trust that is your loved one connecting with you. Sometimes people want a bigger sign, but sometimes you just have to learn to *trust*. See the common theme with the word *trust* when connecting to spirit? I personally have found a correlation between people who trust signs from their loved ones and people who have more physical and visual experiences with their loved ones in spirit. Allowing just does something special to your connection.

We are not usually tuned in to everything around us, especially when driving or at the grocery store. We are usually thinking about what we have to do later, what we are making for dinner, or some chore or errand we need to run. When you see these signs and feel your attention pulled to them, know that your loved one is drawing you to them to connect with you.

Items they may have collected, or hobbies they may have been into, can show up on your path as signs too—something they were passionate about. It could be that they collected coins, cars, stamps, games, or China. Or maybe they were into repairing furniture, gardening, baking, sewing, or fixing up old cars. When you see these things showing up on your path in your day-to-day life, and they make you think of your loved one, it is them. Please know that they are not physically putting these items in your way to remind you of them (I'm also saying this lightly, because spirit has been known to move certain objects, and I've witnessed this firsthand), but are drawing your attention to these things that would have been special to them.

I like to tell people that once our loved ones cross over to the spirit or "soul" form, they are no longer bound by everything heavy, dense, or physical. They are pure energy. How do you get someone's attention if not everyone is tuned in to their mediumship abilities? By drawing their attention to things and items that may have connected you together.

We can all agree that we have had a strange coincidence at one time or another, where we were pulled to look at or listen to something we felt was connected to our loved one on the other side, no matter how much we chose to doubt it. But we too are conscious beings, and they *can* redirect our thoughts about them or to them and connect us with things that remind us of them.

CHAPTER TWENTY-THREE

Being Human

"When you arise in the morning think of what a precious privilege it is to be alive – to breathe, to think, to enjoy and to love."
~ Marcus Aurelius

If there is one thing I can tell you to be aware of, it is that you do not need to be anything other than who you already are to tune in to your spiritual or mediumship self. When I first started opening up to my mediumship, I felt a pressure that was making me feel like I needed to do or be more. Spirit is so closely connected to heaven, God, and the Universe. I was "just" a human, doing human things, and not always perfect, or the highest representation of what my perfect self *could* be. Do yourself a favor, and don't let yourself go there.

You are spirit, and perfect in your own right. Every human goes through life experiences that make them less than perfect. We all have things we need to heal from and that we could be better at. You go through healing at the right time, learning lessons and gaining insight at the right moment for your soul's best timeline. Let's just say that every person on this planet is doing the best they can with the lens they adopted at birth and the experiences they have been through, living and learning through those events the best they know how.

If I got frustrated with my kids, I would catch myself thinking I wasn't a good enough mom and was afraid spirit would judge me. Or I would think spirit would be critical about the fact that I liked to have a glass of wine. I worried that I didn't do enough spiritual practices, like meditating daily, which I thought other mediums did (news flash: they *don't* all meditate). I judged my diet a lot, thinking I needed to eat healthy all the time to have a higher vibration. But we are spirits having a human experience, not the other way around. We are here to learn, grow, and be human. That means truly experiencing all of the beauty life has to offer, good and "bad." That is the beauty of being human, and spirit *wants* you to experience it all!

I have learned that your readings will not be any better in doing these things, despite what *any* teacher tells you. Trust in yourself. If you want to make these changes for yourself, then do them, but don't do them because you think should. I can now laugh at myself thinking I really believed any of that to be true, but it was definitely me unlearning my perfectionist tendencies and seeing just how unhelpful they really were.

I heard once from Esther Hicks, a famous channel, that your thoughts about what you eat are just as important as what you actually eat. If you feel like what you are eating is bad, it will affect you differently than not having any judgment about what you eat, even if it is not the healthiest of foods. Your mental and emotional energies have much more of an impact on your overall health than modern medicine would like you to know about.

Spirit will show up for you and your sitters because they too want to connect to their loved ones. No need to change a thing about yourself. Your diet is fine. You can get upset and frustrated. You can let yourself be human. We are here to live and experience above all. All spirits have been there, and they do not judge. They know better.

One thing I have learned in my mediumship is that when we cross over, we have the chance to review our lives. Looking at the things we judged ourselves too harshly on is one of the things we review. If you want to change your behaviors because you have learned from them, great. If you want to change your diet because you feel called to make a change, that is also great. Just know that spirit holds no expectations of you. You are spirit, and have a soul, and can connect to those on the other side because of that.

I will say that sometimes, spirit will step in to help you get to a better understanding of things, if you have areas in your life that are in need of healing, for example. This is to help you most of all, but you will find it has a cascade effect on those around you in life, and in your readings as well. People naturally go through some sort of healing as they are stepping into their abilities. This is only so you can look at what you have experienced through a different lens and a higher perspective. When you can see your past experiences differently, it will help you give readings without holding judgment or swaying perceptions, because you are no longer held captive by your unhealed self (which is why I recommend detoxing the clutter).

Healing is powerful. It helps you to understand and see that we are not victims at all but learning along our journey. If we've had something bad done to us, it is important to still see them as human and hold some compassion for them when you are able. They more than likely did the best they could with what they knew.

What has been done to you is not your fault, but healing from it is your responsibility. Only you can want that for yourself. It then becomes part of your opportunity in life: to show up the way you would have liked someone to show up for you. Keep in mind that healing and expectations are different. When we feel pressure to be perfect, it's usually showing us that we need to be healed of old beliefs, as we are spirit and already divine. And that, my friends, is why we need connection to spirit: to show us that we are innately already perfect as we are. We do not need perfection, but we do need to understand why we think we do.

CHAPTER TWENTY-FOUR

Reading for Your Loved Ones

"You don't love someone because they are perfect, you love them in spite of the fact that they are not."
~ Jodi Picoult

When your friends and loved ones figure out or find out that you are a psychic and a medium, it can be a double-edged sword. I personally suggest that you do not get too caught up in reading for those you know on a closer level. It can be tempting to want to help those around you and to share your gifts with them, to show them just how helpful your gifts can be, but then we can find ourselves in a helper role that is not healthy for us—or them.

Again, every medium and psychic works differently. Always follow what works for you. However, energy and information that may show up in readings of people who are close to you can be misconstrued, biased by preconceived notions you have gathered about them over time. The readings can be accurate, but they may also be impacted by our judgment or subconscious thoughts. When you read for people you know and connect to them or their loved ones in spirit, the information you get may be skewed or interfered with by current and even previous knowledge you have about them. The information may not come completely from your reading brain. Even if it *is* coming in from spirit or your psychic senses, you may find that you second-guess yourself, which can interfere with the information flowing in. With people you know, you cannot be a complete blank slate and show up without any prior knowledge.

How do you keep your feelings, thoughts, and impressions out of your readings when you truly care about the person you are reading for? This is important to take into account. When you have an emotional connection, it is important not to be swayed by your own thoughts and perceptions. If something sad or emotional comes up, do you hold back, because you don't want to say something for fear of how they might feel or how they might take the information you have to pass on?

Reading for friends and family can cause you to feel pressured to get everything right, to show your loved ones just how your connections work and just how great of a psychic or medium you are. How do you remove yourself from feeling that burden and ensure that it doesn't impact your readings?

I have had many teachers over the years, and every single one recommends that you refer your own close family and friends to other mediums and psychics for this reason. If you have random information come in when you are with your family or friends, you can always share what you are getting or picking up on. Just know that connecting may pull you into things you already know about, which may interfere with a clean reading.

I have had spirit come through for some of my loved ones, but I have found that I may start second-guessing things, comparing them to what I know to be true. I recommend that if you do read for your loved ones, tell spirit they will need to bring through extra information that you have never heard of and are not familiar with. Otherwise, it is not truly an evidential mediumship connection.

I say all this with a touch of caution, because I have met a medium here and there who does read for their loved ones. But in my opinion, they may be passing on bits and pieces of their *own* advice, and things *they* know the sitter may benefit from, without solely tuning in to their energy or loved ones. Pass this discretionary caution on to your friends or family. Be honest and let them know you have prior knowledge before connecting for them.

In contrast, when people you know nothing about show up for a reading, it is safe to pass every piece of information on, because you know it is coming to you from spirit at that moment in time. You can be confident that the information is fresh and trustable.

As I have said all along, you will have to make your own decisions. Just keep in mind true mediumship ethics. Only pass on information that you are *receiving*, not *perceiving*, because that can alter the perception of credibility—not only for you, but for other psychics and mediums. Only you will know and be able to differentiate the information you are picking up on.

CHAPTER TWENTY-FIVE

Questions and Answers from Spirit and Me

"When you realize there is no lacking, the whole world belongs to you."
~ Lao Tzu

The following are common questions that I get along with answers that I've received from spirit. These questions come up frequently in readings and from people who are curious about spirit, our souls, and the afterlife. Some of these questions are from sitters, and some are directly to and from spirit. Spirit's answers are followed by my answers to commonly asked questions.

In making the choice or decision to transition to hospice or comfort care, was it hard to leave your family?

Yes. It was for a little while, but then I had the realization that this was the right choice for me, and I knew that everything would be okay. There was peace about it, and I knew that I could still experience them and connect to them. They would still have each other, and community. They were still here to live and have all of the beautiful experiences they were meant to have. It was difficult, but we still share the same love that we had when I was in the physical. In time, we will be together again.

What have you learned since being gone?

That being on Earth can be hard and challenging at times, but it is where the growth happens. It is a blessing, and something that we *get* to experience. The sights you see, the air you breathe, the hugs you feel—that can all be taken for granted. We can get caught up in this experience or that one thing we are going through, but it truly is an amazing experience that may be overlooked or taken for granted by some. "Heaven on Earth" is a saying people don't entirely understand. People always think of heaven as the experience after we leave our physical bodies, but what if heaven is our experience on Earth as well? Slow down and enjoy the journey! Laughter truly is one of the best medicines. It can heal your soul.

How does the transition process work?

Souls gather when someone passes away to help with the transition process. There is a learning and reorientation that happens. Consider it like a reattuning process. Know that there is no lack of support for the souls transitioning and for the souls left behind on Earth. Family is present from the ethereal realm, which you may not even be aware of until this experience happens to you. We are here and supporting you always. Grief is a difficult process, and that's when people tend to call on us most. Know that we are with you.

When people experience a traumatic passing, do they suffer?

Our souls know no pain. They transition before or during the process and experience death much differently than in the physical. It is a "shedding" that happens, and the soul is separated from the body before they experience any trauma. Please know, we experience a sudden peace upon passing that those left behind do not. If there is one thing you can take from this, it is that we have comfort and an abundance of love waiting on the other side. This is something that is hard to put into words, because you do not experience it in the physical world.

I want something to happen right now. Why isn't it?

People feel the need to always be doing or hurrying through one thing or the next, rushing, thinking they do not have enough time. In hurrying, you tend to lose the experience and joy in the little things, which, when you look back, are life's greatest treasures. Growth is an ongoing process. Principles become teachers and can help us adjust our sails as needed. It doesn't happen overnight, nor would you want it to. You would miss the experience. Enjoy the process, for that is where the joy truly is.

How do I know what choice is right for me?

Choices. We feel pressure and think that we must make the "right choice" in life to be on our "right path." But the truth is that there is no right choice. Life is all about learning and the things you get to experience along the way. The longer you think about the choices you make, the more you get hung up on your ability to experience anything. Just decide and know that you are always on the right path for you. We eventually end up where we are meant to be. One path may take a little longer or be a little shorter than the others, but all choices help us go through what we are learning about at that moment in life. We live and we learn, and that is what life is all about. The journey.

☙

If my loved one passes by suicide, do they get to go to heaven?

I can answer this based on all of my readings for people who have passed by suicide. Yes, yes, and yes. I can promise you that these souls that show up in mediumship readings come through just as strongly, with as many supportive, loving, and healing messages as those that pass by any other means. I have seen many people come for a reading fearing their loved one may not show as if they are away somewhere being punished, and that just isn't so. Upon crossing over, they get the chance to review their life and choices, just as we all do, but they are not punished.

Many religions tell us this, in my belief, out of fear. The thought is that if we scare people away from doing certain things, they won't do them. But we all know that everyone lives and learns through their own experiences, and fear doesn't always keep people from doing things. I really dislike this teaching though, because I know otherwise, and someone dealing with the sudden, unexpected passing of a loved one is going through a difficult enough time as it is. They do not need to go through the extra fear that we will not reconnect with those loved ones in heaven, because it simply isn't so. They are learning and growing on the other side, just as we all will.

How do mediums connect with pets or loved ones who don't speak the same language?

In my readings, spirit will show up, and I hear a word or so in their language, which tells me they speak a different language, as validation for my sitter. Everything else then comes through hearing, seeing, and feeling, just the same as someone who speaks the same language as me. Pets work the same way. They absolutely have souls as well! I see pets and pick up on health issues or things they loved doing, just the same as humans. This is because language is universal on the other side. We are all souls and communicate the same way, even though it may seem confusing. It's all the same. We are no longer bound by race, religion, ethnicity, etc. Those are simply identifiers for our human life.

Do you have any advice for a parent losing a child?

This can be the most difficult of all losses. Please know that even though the grief process is a difficult one, the soul of your child is not suffering. All experiences happen for a reason, even though we may not understand them at the time. The soul of the child more than likely knew that they might not be here for long. This doesn't make the experience any easier for their family but know that there are life lessons we all experience that are for a purpose. They are still around you and sharing your love from heaven. Most children are very wise or old souls and come into our lives as teachers in one way or another.

We think that as parents, or with age, we know more. This isn't always true. Isn't it when we need it most that our children say things or show us through their actions that we are the ones truly learning from our experiences with *them*? Nothing can ever replace your child, and nothing is meant to. It is in our grief that we are reminded just how much love they brought into our lives. Maybe that is their purpose in our lives. I find that in many readings, children will come through as "joy guides," helping people to remember that life is short and we are meant to live in a happy state of being, just as they would have done. I also think of them as helper souls and find that they may help other younger souls from the other side. They truly are a gift from God. The love they bring is incomparable.

Can spirits on the other side see everything I do, even in the shower or during intimate moments, etc.?

Yes, they absolutely can. And I can tell you from experience that prior to reading, I've had spirits start coming in while I am in the shower. However, that doesn't mean they care one lick about you being naked, and that's most definitely not why they've shown up. It's more about the state of mind you are in at the time, and if it allows for some relaxation. In a calmer state, you become more receptive, which makes you able to better pick up on the spirits around you.

Spirit is exactly that—a spirit—and doesn't care about the physical things in life, such as how you look, your status, or the money you earn. They have a much higher understanding. You are simply a vessel they can connect with. I have even received information from spirit—specifically that a man was a fireman in life and earned a medal for his rescues—while taking a shower. Granted, I was about to do a group reading and had already let spirit know I was ready to connect (oh, the life of a medium!). I simply share this with you so that you understand they don't care about being with you while you're naked or on the toilet or doing anything personal. It's about relaying information and the state you're in while receiving it.

My loved one and I weren't getting along when they passed. I am sorry for how we left things. Do they still carry resentment or anger?

No. They absolutely do not. When crossing into heaven, spirits leave behind all heavy human emotions, such as anger, hate, fear, regret, resentment, etc. This is because heaven is full of love and higher knowing that we do not experience here on Earth. In the life review process, they get to experience and understand the emotions they held onto in life. They get to really see if they were helpful or not and how those emotions may have held them back, and why or how they may have been able to handle their emotions differently. I can only describe this as a "true understanding." They understand and see things from a different perspective that doesn't carry all the baggage we do here on Earth.

I didn't get to say goodbye to my loved one. Can you do this for me?

Yes, I can. However, you do not need me to. Spirit can hear, see, and feel everything you do. They are no longer limited to the physical and can be in multiple places at once. They can hear your thoughts and see everything you are doing. They already know your thoughts and feelings around their departure. They know all of your regrets and all of the things you wish you had been able to say. You can communicate with them on your own. You do not need a medium to do this for you. I know this to be true, because spirit is always bringing up occurrences in your life during readings to let you know that they are aware of what is going on. This is confirmation that they are experiencing this along with you.

I had an experience that prevented me from a really bad, almost near-death experience. Was this spirit?

I believe you already know this answer. Did it feel guided, or like you were spared from something? Were you headed out the door when you felt a nudge to go back and check something, which made you take a few seconds longer, delaying your departure just enough to prevent you being somewhere where something bad or tragic happened? Did you hear something that startled you, then feel pulled to slow down, or turn in a different direction, only to seconds later witness a car accident that would have been fatal to you if you hadn't listened? Spirit connects to the average individual much more than you realize; you just aren't aware that it's coming from outside of you, because you aren't aware of how that experience feels. Just know that everything happens for a reason!

Who helps us in/through life?

From my experience, I can tell you that I have had souls' step in to help me whom I have had no relation to. We all have spirit guides and angels that assist us through life—challenges, growth spurts, all the good and tough times alike. Our own loved ones also step in and are around us. To me, they feel and look different, so it's easy to determine who is who.

I see spirits in my dreams as well. Often, these are people I know and had a relationship with or a connection to in my life before they passed on. Sometimes I dream of the same spirits over and over again, whom I do not know. They help me work on things that I am growing through in life, and I call these my spirit guides and angels.

I hear words as well throughout the day that relate to things I am experiencing. I get strong nudges and feel or see things, knowing they are coming from someone bigger than me that are not my loved ones in spirit. I know they do not come from me, because they are much smarter words than I personally use, or they are in a different language that I have to Google. These spirits feel and look different. They have a much bigger energy. But they are always kind, inspirational, leading, or thought-provoking.

One way to help us understand who our helpers or spirit guides are, is to pay attention to our dreams and things that we are subconsciously drawn to. Is it a certain culture you are drawn to, or a particular place or destination? Maybe a specific job or experience you feel pulled toward? These messages give us hints about who our guides are. The more you pay attention, the more you will see them show up, and you will understand who they are.

Keep in mind that they can help us, but we have free will. So, unless you ask for help, or you are in a situation that could change your life, they generally leave it up to you to reach out. They cannot make decisions for us. It is our life to live. They are simply here to help us on our journey. The same goes for angels. They don't just interject, unless they feel you really need help. They have a higher understanding of the bigger picture, and the seemingly difficult things we are going through are to help us overcome things in life. I suggest asking for help or support, and you will start to see just how much these souls have to offer us. It may completely change your life and understanding of just how much we are supported by the spirit realm.

My loved one was not a nice person. They did a lot of wrong, and I'm worried they might not be in heaven. How do I know if they are in heaven?

This might not be a popular concept (you can make up your own mind; don't let me sway your beliefs), but I don't believe there is a hell. This is something I believe humans have created to try to get other humans to behave in a certain manner. I believe we all go to the same place, full of love and understanding. We may have very different levels of learning to do, but we all go to a heaven-like place. People may do what we think of as "bad things," but all of our souls are pure and made of unconditional love. Even souls who do horrible things here on Earth teach others something of value, like how we should work together more, or simply how *not* to be.

I believe that before we come into this life, we choose who our parents will be and know certain situations we will be encountering in life, though not all, because of us having free will. We choose certain life experiences for learning, growing, and healing purposes. The lessons are important. Heaven is so full of love that it is hard for our souls to grow as much there, because we don't encounter the same challenges that we do here on Earth, which is precisely why we come here.

We deal with far more of what people label "hell on Earth"—murders, war, hate, all that stuff—here on Earth. I believe that certain souls who created a lot of havoc here on Earth, after having a life review and seeing how they impacted others, will be reincarnated and experience something similar for their soul's growth. Please keep in mind that we can experience things like heaven here on Earth too. Spirit has told me this much after I had a long conversation with someone about the suffering people experience while on earth. Love, children, family, friends, dancing, the beautiful sights, smells, and experiences we can have with our human senses... It truly is all about perception. Spirit has said that what we perceive as good or bad isn't quite so in spirit's eyes. If something has been done in life that you perceive as bad, but you or others learn from it, overcome it, or change it and make it good, then was it truly bad at all?

An example would be that someone grew up with an abusive or absent parent. But if that person then grows up and becomes a loving and present parent, you quite literally have turned this bad experience into a good one. You've changed things for generations to come. You overcame it, turned tragedy into triumph. Keep in mind that some things can truly happen that leave us wondering how such horrible and bad things may happen. I don't have answers to everything, or I wouldn't be here in "Earth School," learning alongside you. I just trust that somehow, spirit knows the bigger picture, and I trust that we experience certain things for a reason. I may not know, but I trust that my soul and source do.

Epilogue

When you choose to tune in to spirit, you will feel like your eyes have been shut to so many things in life. Remember that we are spirit having a physical experience, not the other way around. Connecting to these innate abilities can be helpful, not only for you, but for so many others. Remember that you can do this for yourself or others, and that you do not have to use these abilities professionally if you choose not to. Only you will know if this is something you want to develop or not, and if you want to do it professionally. Again, everyone's journey is going to be different.

This path to developing your abilities will push and challenge you, but you will find so much healing and growth. It will be well worth it. Helping to be a communicator for the spirit world quite literally brings knowledge of heaven to earth, bringing knowledge of the afterlife and enlightening others' lives. My wish is to encourage, inspire, and help you on your journey of developing your own gifts, so we can do this together.

Please remember how important it is to use your ethics in always delivering your messages with truth, and respecting spirit and their families who are grieving. People count on and trust us to do so. Go easy on yourself during development, as you are learning and growing. Try to connect with like-minded people, as they will always encourage you to grow further.

You will know what teachers to turn to in your development, because they will always feel right. Remember that even if you find a teacher whom you don't mesh well with, they too will be a teacher for you, even if to only learn how you do *not* want to be.

When you run into struggles during your development, remember your best and most evidential readings. That will bring you back to your confidence. And remember that we are always learning. We are never finished with our spiritual journey. Spirit is always helping and supporting our growth.

You can also reach out to me, if you are interested in taking my development classes, at sarahjanik.com.

Wishing you many beautiful connections in your future.

Lots of love from me and spirit.

Acknowledgements

First and foremost, I would like to thank all my family. Coming out and letting the world know you talk to dead people isn't the easiest task, but thankfully, I was able to do so with so much support and love from my family and friends.

I most definitely want to thank my clients, who have supported me and my spiritual practice since day one. Connecting to your loved ones has truly opened my heart and mind to the other world so much more than I ever thought possible. The love, laughter, tears, and stories in connecting to and getting to know your loved ones has given me so much joy.

I also want to thank spirit and the knowledge you have helped me to remember. It is through our connections that I have been able to perceive the bigger picture and remember that we are so much more than merely human.

I am blessed beyond measure to have all of you in my life.